Gallatin 200

This statue of Albert Gallatin stands just outside the United States Treasury Building in Washington, D.C.

Gallatin
200

*A Time Line History Celebrating the Bicentennial
of
Gallatin, Tennessee*

EDITED BY
WALTER DURHAM AND GLENDA MILLIKEN

TENNESSEE HERITAGE LIBRARY

Copyright 2002 by Walter T. Durham and Glenda B. Milliken

All rights reserved. Written permission must be secured from the publisher to use or reproduce any part of this book, except for brief quotations in critical reviews or articles.

Printed in the United States of America

0 6   0 5   0 4   0 3   0 2   1   2   3   4   5

Library of Congress Catalog Card Number: 2001099119

ISBN: 1-57736-258-6

Cover design by Gary Bozeman

Cover photos by Gallatin 200's photo editor, Allen Haynes

238 Seaboard Lane • Franklin, Tennessee 37067
800-321-5692
www.providencepubcorp.com

Rose Mont.   Courtesy of Sumner County Archives

The Gallatin Bicentennial Celebration Committee, Inc.

Walter T. Durham, President
E. Ray Bowles Sr., Vice President
Glenda Milliken, Secretary
Bob Morgan, Treasurer

Donna Belote
Dale Bennett
Lucy Bradley
Velma Brinkley
Rev. Everton Campbell
Tracy Carman
Jamie Clifton
Mike Cook
Lee Curtis
John Garrott
Kay Hurt
Bill Kirkpatrick

Reggie Mudd
Peter Odom
George Offitt Sr.
David Parsons
Tommy Perkins
Rev. David Randolph
Jim Svoboda
James Thomas
Kenneth Thomson
Grace A. Tomkins
Ralph Webster
Mayor Don Wright

THE MAYOR'S HONORARY COMMITTEE

This Honorary Committee has been chosen by Mayor Wright from former mayors who served during the period 1974-1997. Listed in order of their election, they are:
Fred A. Kelly, Byron Charlton, John Hancock, David Schreiner,
Dick Dempsey, Tommy Garrott, Robert W. Lankford.

By Allen Haynes

Looking eastward from Public Square on Main Street, 2001.

Contents

FOREWORD	ix–xii
PREFACE AND ACKNOWLEDGMENTS	xv–xvi
PART I	1
1. A Celebration	3
2. The Inner Workings	8
3. The Voters' Choice	13
PART II	25
4. Time Line History, Gallatin 1802–2002	26
Epilogue	115
APPENDIX	117
A. These Men and Women Deliver for Gallatin	117
B. Congratulatory Letters	120
Congratulations from Senator Bill Frist	121
Congratulations from Senator Fred Thompson	122
Congratulations from Congressman Bart Gordon	123
Congratulations from Governor Don Sundquist	124
Congratulations from Mayor Bill Purcell	125
Congratulations from County Executive Tom Marlin	126
SELECTED BIBLIOGRAPHY	127
INDEX	131

City of Gallatin, Tennessee

Proclamation

WHEREAS, James Trousdale, whose son William was later Governor of Tennessee, was one of the first settlers of Sumner County; and

WHEREAS, Commissioners Samuel Donelson, Shadrack Nye, James Wilson, Charles Donaho, and Major Thomas Murray purchased 42 ½ acres from Trousdale's North Carolina land grant #1 and founded Gallatin; and

WHEREAS, On February 26, 1802, with the first sale of town lots Gallatin became the seat of government for Sumner County; and

WHEREAS, The name, Gallatin, honors Albert Gallatin, a Swiss born Pennsylvania Congressman and Statesman who was instrumental in Tennessee gaining admission to the Union in 1796; and

WHEREAS, Contributions of Gallatin residents – past and present – have not only been significant to the history of our fine city but to the history of Sumner County, the State of Tennessee, and the United States of America; and

WHEREAS, February 26, 2002 marks the City of Gallatin's 200th Birthday; and

WHEREAS, In honor of Gallatin's bicentennial, a time capsule will be buried on the front lawn of City Hall for future Gallatin residents to open in 100 years;

NOW, THEREFORE, I, Don Wright, Mayor of the City of Gallatin, Tennessee do hereby proclaim the entire year of 2002 as

Gallatin's Bicentennial

And encourage all citizens to take part in the year-long festival honoring our fine city.

IN WITNESS WHEREOF, I have hereunto set my hand and caused to be affixed the official seal of the City of Gallatin, Tennessee, this 1st day of January 2002.

_____
DON WRIGHT, MAYOR

Foreword

PERSPECTIVES FROM THE MAYOR'S OFFICE

By Mayor Don Wright

Being elected mayor of a two-centuries-old city the size of Gallatin is comparable to inheriting a $30 million company where the mayor is the C.E.O. and our seven city council members are the board of directors. It most certainly is an exciting and challenging proposition.

Created by the Tennessee General Assembly and established as the seat of Sumner County in 1802, Gallatin was immediately on its way to the solid Middle Tennessee prominence that it now enjoys. Its potential was so widely recognized in its first decade that according to one of my favorite stories, geographers in England thought it was outstripping Nashville. An American gazetteer, published in London in 1820, identified Nashville this way: "Nashville. An important Cumberland River port 27 miles downstream from Gallatin." We still feel that way today.

Unlike many municipalities of comparable size (23,230 men, women, and children in the U.S. census of 2000), Gallatin is a fully self-contained city. Our Electric Department, offering the second lowest rates in the state, has an outstanding service record with no brownouts and very few minor incidents or downtime where loss of power occurs. Our Public Utilities Department operates and maintains systems that distribute water and natural gas to customers and delivers sewage to a modern disposal plant. Offering customers the lowest rates in Middle Tennessee, the department is continually expanding its capacity. It presently serves not only Gallatin but also several outlying communities.

Our Sanitation Department, which utilizes the latest type of automated equipment, picks up household refuse, trash, garbage, and debris, and is regarded as a model for cities in Sumner and surrounding counties.

The Sumner County Resource Authority, a cooperative venture with Hendersonville and Sumner County, generates the collected refuse into salable steam and electricity. It is a great economic development tool that helps bring new consumers, business, and industry to Gallatin.

Although Sumner Regional Medical Center and the Sumner County Airport, both at Gallatin, were county initiatives, the city has cooperated with both entities as they have expanded to meet the needs of the area. Local economic development has been a principal sustaining factor for both.

The city participated financially in the establishment of Volunteer State Community College which educates over six thousand students per year. That performance assures that our businesses and industries will have an abundance of well-prepared employees.

We have a terrific civic-recreational center that has been touted as the ultimate sports complex in Middle Tennessee, and a parks system that is coveted by communities all across the South. Our six hundred acres of parks are comprised of sixteen baseball and/or softball fields, two football fields, sixteen soccer fields, an eighteen-hole disc golf course, outdoor pool with water slide, six tennis courts, six basketball courts, and the old City

GALLATIN 200

City Hall.

By Allen Haynes

Cemetery where each year the Sumner County Museum hosts a historical cemetery tour that draws hundreds of people.

Long Hollow Golf Course is a state-of-the-art eighteen-hole public golf course with a historic home as a clubhouse, sixty-eight new golf carts, and a well-stocked pro shop. The course is a beautifully manicured green blanket that covers a former landfill dumpsite. Its very existence shows the forethought of those mayors and councilpersons in the past and challenges those of us who serve today to be equally as innovative.

Our Public Works Department is second to none. Dealing with needs wherever they exist, the department paves city streets and sidewalks and addresses long-term problems and opportunities such as flood control, stormwater drains and detention ponds, and traffic signals and signs. The department also responds to the multitude of citizen questions and requests that arise on a daily basis in any municipality where change is constant.

The changing face of the city is directly related to planning and economic development. We have a very professional, well-qualified Planning and Codes Department and an equally exceptional seven-person Planning Commission that is appointed by the mayor. Our newly implemented Economic Development Agency seeks not only to sustain employment at a high level but to help build Gallatin's tax base. The daily responsibilities of these departments are to assure and guide Gallatin's growth in the right direction with proper planning and timely execution. All one has to do is look around our city at the new businesses, restaurants, residential developments, and industry to see the results of their work.

We are extremely proud of our well-equipped, professionally trained Police and Fire Departments. The effective work of the police chief and his officers has resulted in Gallatin's overall crime rate being among the lowest in the state. We have two modern fire halls and a third on the drawing board. The fire chief and his department boast a rare commodity in Middle Tennessee: a one-hundred-foot aerial boom truck which provides access to the top of Gallatin's tallest buildings. The truck is a great step forward in fire safety.

Gallatin's Three Star Chamber of Commerce, the Greater Gallatin, Inc., and the Downtown Merchants Association work tirelessly to enhance the past, present, and future of the city. Gallatin is home to the Sumner County Museum, the Sumner County Archives, numerous antebellum plantation houses and sites, and two historic districts, one of which encompasses the town square. Indeed, history has been good to our city, and we must do our part to see that our heritage is not lost in these fast-changing, exciting times.

The mayor and city council support and approve various community enhancement grants that assist in delivering aid to all levels of Gallatin citizenry. We believe that public welfare and quality of life issues are of the utmost importance to our people and community, and our public servants would be irresponsible not to join hands with the private sector in these civic service areas. Handled properly, a city–private corporation partnership that promotes public good is an excellent investment of Gallatin tax dollars.

Of course, providing those many quality-of-life services can be achieved only by insuring that they are adequately funded. Therefore, it is pertinent that each year the mayor, city council, and city department heads compile, review, amend, and adopt a budget on July 1 that falls within the perimeter of our annual expendable revenue. In other words, we must present a balanced budget.

The budget process is long and arduous, taking three to four months or more to complete and often requires many special-called meetings. The necessary revenue to meet our budget is acquired through three main sources: sales tax (which we split with the county); real estate (property tax); and various privilege taxes such as building permits. As a precaution, in the event of unforeseen major expenses or crisis such as a downturn in the economy or a devastating storm, it is the practice of our elected officials to maintain a reserve, or as we call it "a rainy day fund," that at all times is equivalent to at least 20 percent of the city's operating expenses.

Wynnewood.

Courtesy of Tennessee State Library and Archives

GALLATIN 200

Fire Headquarters.

By Allen Haynes

After the budget has been adopted by the city council, the actual funding of the city's many financial obligations demands the daily attention of the mayor's office and the Finance Department. Every tax dollar received—and where it goes—is carefully monitored throughout the entire year. Gallatin's revenue and disbursements not only have a direct impact on projects and programs that take place today or in the immediate future, but they also dictate to some degree the far-reaching avenue our city will travel throughout the remainder of this century.

Gallatin, in all its departments, employs some 330 persons, each of whom has a role in bringing municipal services to the public. The human needs of a force this size requires professional expertise and a common sense approach in all of the matters that affect not only their employment but their daily lives as well. The mayor and council expect a lot from our city employees, and our employees have a right to expect the same from us. We must be alert to their working conditions, be certain that we recognize the contributions they make, and treat them with the dignity and respect that we covet for ourselves.

All of us in government must recognize that the only power we have is that which is delegated to us by the people. Trying to make the relationships between the city and the public as positive as possible is a responsibility and duty that the mayor, the council, and all other employees of the city embrace on an hour-by-hour basis. It is extremely fulfilling when our collective efforts produce satisfactory results for them.

What do I, as mayor, see when I look out our City Hall window at the town I regard so highly? I see people walking our streets in safety; I see bustling businesses; I see our past proudly preserved; I see churches where large and small congregations worship in the religious tradition of their choice; I see a city where folks are looking at the far horizon, unafraid to take a step in that direction. I see Gallatin, yesterday, today, and tomorrow—and taking all of the above into consideration, one can begin to understand the pride, the excitement, and the humbling experience of being mayor of a city like Gallatin, Tennessee. I am grateful for this opportunity to serve.

State of Tennessee

THE SENATE

SENATE JOINT RESOLUTION NO. 128

By Senator Jo Ann Graves
and
Representatives Tim Garrett, Diane Black and Mike McDonald

A RESOLUTION
To honor and commend the members of the Gallatin Bicentennial Committee as they prepare to
celebrate the founding of historic Gallatin.

WHEREAS, It is fitting that this General Assembly should recognize those citizens who take great pride in their Tennessee heritage and make great efforts to celebrate their history; and

WHEREAS, The members of the Gallatin Bicentennial Committee are just such citizens; they are currently engrossed in diligent preparations for the celebration of their beloved town's 200th birthday; and

WHEREAS, On the 6th of November 1801, the General Assembly of the State of Tennessee passed an act naming commissioners and directing those commissioners to select a site for the County Seat of Sumner County; and

WHEREAS, The act further instructed the commissioners to plan the layout of the town and then sell lots at public sale to the highest bidders; and

WHEREAS, The act called for the town to be named "Gallatin"; and

WHEREAS, The commissioners, in full compliance with the provisions of the act, conducted a public sale of town lots on the 26th of February 1802, and thus they created the Town of Gallatin; and

WHEREAS, Citizens of Gallatin plan to observe their city's 200th birthday throughout the year 2002; and

WHEREAS, The Honorable Mayor of Gallatin, Don Wright, has appointed a committee of stalwart citizens to serve on the Gallatin Bicentennial Committee; and

WHEREAS, The Committee will plan and coordinate appropriate activities to celebrate their town's past, present, and future throughout its bicentennial year; and

WHEREAS, This General Assembly is pleased to honor citizens who hail from one of Tennessee's most historic towns; now, therefore,

BE IT RESOLVED BY THE SENATE OF THE ONE HUNDRED SECOND GENERAL ASSEMBLY OF THE STATE OF TENNESSEE, THE HOUSE OF REPRESENTATIVES CONCURRING, That we hereby extend our congratulations and best wishes to the Mayor, City Council, Bicentennial Committee, and Citizens of Gallatin as they prepare to celebrate the founding of the County Seat of the fifth oldest County in the State of Tennessee.

Adopted: March 29, 2001

Speaker of the Senate

Speaker of the House of Representatives

Governor

Joint Resolutions of the General Assembly signed by Governor, Speakers, and Secretary of State.

By Allen Haynes

Looking northward from Public Square on Water Street, 2001.

Preface &
Acknowledgments

This commemorative book is for all those who care about Gallatin, Tennessee, and about small American cities in general. It is at once personal and parochial. It is about Gallatin people and about this place, and it only scratches the surface. An essay could be written about almost any line in the time line history and volumes about some. But let this be a beginning.

No book is exclusively the work of one or two persons. *Gallatin 200* is the work of many including not only those whose names appear in the credits but hundreds of others who have joined spirits to make the Bicentennial Celebration of 2002 a rousing reality.

Lest we forget, there would be no two hundredth birthday of our city had it not been for those diligent commissioners who staked out and sold the first town lots. From that beginning Gallatin grew slowly and cautiously for the next one hundred and fifty years. During the last fifty years, however, its growth has accelerated into a much livelier pace.

When the bicentennial planning committee first met on January 19, 2001, we agreed unanimously that we were glad to be living in this town rooted for two hundred years in American history. Other agreements came just as easily. We must celebrate the two hundred years, although not all years were as noble as we might have liked. We must take stock of where we are at the beginning of the third century and, as individual citizens, look ahead to share our hopes and dreams with elected officials at all levels of government. We agreed it was time to review our history and use it in the elusive but important task of understanding how we arrived where we are.

Following the Bicentennial celebrations of the United States (1776–1976), the county of Sumner (1786–1986), and the state of Tennessee (1796–1996), a similar Gallatin observance required broad public support. And we found it. Everywhere we turned our fellow citizens were ready to celebrate and learn more about this town with its proud past and promising future.

Serious preparation for observing the two hundredth birthday all began when the planning committee appointed by Mayor Don Wright reorganized into the Gallatin Bicentennial Celebration Committee, Inc., a bona fide not-for-profit entity. Representing a broad cross section of citizens, members of the committee determined at the outset to make the entire activity inclusive of the total community.

A sampling of the private sector indicated solid financial support for the undertaking and on April 24, 2001, the city council appropriated fifty thousand dollars as its vital vote of confidence. Responses received as of this date suggest that contributions from the private sector will exceed sixty thousand dollars.

It was decided early in the committee's deliberations that instead of a single event lasting a day or two, the celebration would extend throughout the year. A number of events would be scheduled to occur between the beginning on Unity Day, January 21, 2002, and the ending on Thanksgiving Eve with a town-wide Union Thanksgiving service. The midyear high point will be an expanded July 4 celebration at the Municipal City Park in cooperation with the Gallatin Chamber of Commerce.

GALLATIN 200

As this book goes to press prior to the year 2002, it is not possible for it to include acknowledgments of the gifts of private and corporate donors nor the contribution of time volunteered by so many. We regret, also, that we cannot list the many events that will occur between the beginning in mid-January and the end on Thanksgiving Eve. All of this information and more will appear appropriately during 2002.

At this stage special recognition must go to those who committed the initial funds to the undertaking: Mayor Don Wright, Vice Mayor Deotha Malone, Aldermen Ed Mayberry, Daryl Holt, Robert Lea, John Alexander, Craig Hayes, and Paul Perry. The counsel and advice of City Attorney Joe H. Thompson was invaluable. Recorder Connie Kittrell and her staff compiled from the earliest records the list of elected city officials that appears in this book, and Tammy DeMeio in the mayor's office has helped often and tirelessly.

We can and must express appreciation for their early cooperation to four of our principal institutions: Volunteer State Community College; the Sumner County Regional Medical Center; the Gallatin TVA Fossil Plant; and the *News Examiner*. Persons associated with these institutions at all levels have cooperated in numerous ways.

As we moved this book from concept to press in a period of six months, we needed the support of the local history community, and it was there. Consultation with history regulars John Garrott, James W. Thomas, Kenneth Thomson, Velma Brinkley, and Nathan Harsh has been extremely helpful. The staff of the Tennessee State Library was alert and served us promptly. The capable assistance of Cora Harper and Ann Ross of the Sumner County Archives was graciously extended on the many occasions when we needed it. Encouraging us at every turn were the leaders of the Rose Mont Restoration Foundation, Inc.; the Bledsoe's Lick Historical Association, Inc.; Historic Cragfont, Inc.; and the Sumner County Historical Society.

The editors acknowledge their responsibilities in this project. The work of Allen Haynes and his camera appears throughout the book as do certain older photographs from his extensive collections of Sumner County images. Glenda Milliken researched most of the time line data and prepared the book for publication. With the exception of the foreword written by Mayor Wright and the comments from the other elected officials in chapter two, Walter Durham wrote the text. The editors gladly share any credit or blame that readers may bestow.

Walter T. Durham
Editor

Glenda Milliken
Associate Editor

Allen Haynes
Photographer and Photo Editor

Gallatin, Tennessee
November 19, 2001

Part One

CHAPTER ONE

A Celebration

The celebration of the two hundredth year in the life of any city in the United States of America can be an occasion for joy, a time to review its history, and a time to look ahead. In the case of Gallatin, Tennessee, there is much to acknowledge by joyous celebration, examining a proud history, and looking ahead to a future limited only by the timidity of our dreams.

On its two hundredth birthday, we celebrate the cultural diversity of this city's people. A few decades ago, descendants from European Caucasians and African blacks constituted almost the entire population, but in 2002 there are significant numbers of immigrants from south of the border as well as others, notably from southeast Asia. To meet these changing times, one of the city's largest employers has created a diversity council through which employees seek to identify and understand the strengths that can be shared in a diverse population. Such an approach could be an example for us all.

We celebrate the veneration that our people have always shown toward education at all levels. From the earliest times of settlement, teaching children has been a high priority. For about a century, private schools were dominant. The one-hundred-year evolution of the Gallatin Female Academy of the 1820s into Sumner Female Academy in the 1830s into Howard Female Institute in the 1850s and finally into Howard College is a compelling example of local commitment to educating young women. Transmontania, the boys school of 1806, closed its doors during the Civil War, but reopened afterward. It was succeeded by Gallatin Male Seminary which by the turn of the century was followed in order by Hawkins School, Williams School, and Gallatin Private Institute (G.P. I.).

District or common schools operated throughout the 1800s with unpredictable and modest public funding. The advent of a Gallatin Board of Education in 1884 was the beginning of public schools of the type seen here today, although the city system yielded to a countywide system around 1950.

During the early 1920s, Howard Female College closed, its financial resources exhausted. About the same time, the last of the private boys' schools, G.P.I., closed for the same reason. The public schools then shouldered the full burden of educating the young of Gallatin. Private schools began to reappear when Sumner Academy, a coed independent elementary school was opened in 1973 and, soon afterward, College Heights Christian Academy began enrolling students.

Although in 1909 there was widespread indifference toward having Gallatin chosen for the location of the newly created Middle Tennessee State Normal College that evolved into Middle Tennessee State University, local citizens worked successfully sixty-five years later to bring the proposed Volunteer State Community College here. The presence of the college has added greatly to local interest in and support for higher education.

We celebrate an old and historic town. It is situated on land that was a Native American hunting ground shared by the Cherokee, Shawnee, and Chickasaw until colonial settlers began to push across the mountains to the valley of the Cumberland River during the latter years of the American Revolution. With independence from Great Britain, the state of North Carolina possessed the region until ceding it

GALLATIN 200

to the federal government in 1789. The next year Congress declared it to be the Territory of the United States South of the River Ohio. When the territory in its entirety was converted into the state of Tennessee in 1796, it became Tennessee ground and has been so ever since.

On its two hundredth birthday, Gallatin is proud of its American heritage, although its beginnings were uncertain and undoubtedly controversial. When the state of Tennessee was created, Sumner County was nine years old but did not have a town designated as its county seat. Taking note of the situation, the General Assembly passed an act appointing five commissioners to locate a site and three trustees to purchase it, to erect a courthouse, prison and stocks, and to establish a town. Section III of the statute named the town Ca Ira, a rallying cry of the French Revolution meaning "it will go on."

Notified that the commissioners had been unable to agree on a site, the General Assembly repealed the act on October 2, 1797, and passed a new one. This time there were eleven commissioners and three trustees. To guide them, the act called for locating the town along a line drawn from Mansker's Fort to Bledsoe's Lick running at all times equidistant from the river. Although they devoted two years to the task, the larger group of commissioners could not reach agreement.

In 1799 the General Assembly repealed the act of 1797 and appointed five new commissioners with the combined powers heretofore given to both commissioners and trustees. They were to locate the site within a mile and a half of a north-south line dividing the county into equal sections east and west. This time the town was to be named Rutherford to honor the Revolutionary War Gen. Griffith Rutherford of North Carolina who had moved from east of the Appalachians to Sumner County a few years before. The commissioners of 1799 fared no better than those who had preceded them; they could not agree on a suitable location.

After repealing the act of 1799, the General Assembly made yet another effort to provide for the county seat of Sumner. On November 6, 1801, the fourth act on this subject appointed five new commissioners, introduced the name "Gallatin" in honor of the western Pennsylvania Congressman Albert Gallatin, and specified that the town site be chosen from one of three set forth. The three areas were clustered so close that they are all within the bounds of twenty-first century Gallatin. James Trousdale's North Carolina Land Grant No. 1 happened to fall in the center of the three, and the commissioners promptly purchased forty-two and one-half acres of it. They laid out the county seat town and sold the first lots on February 26, 1802. The site is more particularly described as lying at latitude 36° 16´ north and longitude 86° 18´ west from London.

The sale actually marked the beginning of Gallatin as it fulfilled the mandate of the General Assembly, a closure that prior commissioners had been unable to reach. At that time there was only one building, the home of James Trousdale, standing within the town.

The challenges of growing from one house surrounded by unimproved lots, streets, and alleys into a county seat town seem to have fed the appetites of both those who were looking for a place of permanent settlement and others who stopped over, biding their time to move farther westward. Settlers who arrived during the first twenty years built and sustained the town. Although they shared in community responsibilities, the townsfolk held tightly to their frontier sense of independence.

At two hundred the city salutes Abraham Alfonse Albert Gallatin who was born January 29, 1761, in Geneva, Switzerland. Jean Gallatin, his father, died in 1765 and his mother Mme. Gallatin-Rolaz died five years later, leaving Albert an orphan. His grandparents afforded him liberal support until he completed his education at the Academy of Geneva in 1779.

Albert Gallatin immigrated to the United States in 1780 and, after a few years in the East, moved to Pennsylvania. There he was a member of the state Constitutional Convention of 1789–1790 and served in the state legislature from 1790 to 1792. In 1795 he was elected to the United States Congress from western Pennsylvania. It was while in that body in 1796 that he took an active part in winning admission to the Union for the new state of Tennessee. For that assistance, the grateful citizens of Tennessee named the county seat of Sumner to honor him. In congressional debates, his reasoned defense of the First Amendment that protects the rights to free speech and free press still draws the attention of scholars. John Seigenthaler, founder of the First Amendment Center at Vanderbilt University, insists that Gallatin is a "First Amendment hero" not only for his leadership on the floor of the House of Representatives but also for his effective advocacy behind the scenes.

A Time Line History Celebrating the Bicentennial of Gallatin, Tennessee

In 1801 President Thomas Jefferson appointed Albert Gallatin Secretary of the Treasury where, reappointed by President James Madison, he remained until 1813. From 1813 to 1829, he held several diplomatic assignments including the treaty negotiations that concluded the War of 1812 (Treaty of Ghent) and ambassadorships to France and Great Britain.

Gallatin had been interested in the habits and culture of Native Americans from the time of his arrival in Boston in 1780. In 1836 he published an essay "A Synopsis of the Indian Tribes within the United States east of the Rocky Mountains and in the British and Russian possessions in North America." He was the key figure in organizing the American Ethnological Society of New York in 1842. The society published its first volume in 1845, three hundred pages of which are devoted to Gallatin's "Notes on the Semi-Civilized Nations of Mexico, Yucatan, and Central America." His many accomplishments did not include a visit to the town named for him, however.

Albert Gallatin died in New York in 1849. His Pennsylvania farm home Friendship Hill was designated a National Historic Landmark in 1965. Since 1980 it has been managed by the National Park Service of the Department of the Interior.

Whether they remained at home or went west, local folk of the early 1800s were westerners of mind and spirit and hawkish in their desire to defend and/or expand the nation's boundaries. They volunteered readily whenever called for service in the military. Local volunteers participated in the War of 1812, the Seminole War of 1836, the Mexican War, the Civil War, and the Spanish American War—five in the nineteenth century. Gallatin men and women took up active duty in a like number of wars during the twentieth century: World War I, World War II, the Korean War, the Vietnam War, and the Persian Gulf War.

During its first 125 years, Gallatin was primarily a retail trade center for a rural, agricultural region. Beginning in the 1920s, factories to process milk, cream, and tobacco products appeared. Two shoe manufacturing plants came at the depth of the Great Depression, and after World War II, Gallatin attracted industries that produced a variety of metal products including office furniture, windows and doors, locks and hardware, and powdered metals. Factories sprang up that crafted home furniture, garments, mattresses, hair dryers, trailers, and mobile homes. Still others printed telephone directories, newspaper inserts, and magazines;

By Allen Haynes
TVA Gallatin Fossil Plant, full elevation view of main complex.

warehoused and distributed casual clothing throughout the Southeast; stamped metal parts; did precision casting; and produced tools and dies to order. Since 1956, the Tennessee Valley Authority (TVA) has generated electricity using steam turbines at its fossil-fueled Gallatin plant. Beginning in 1981, the Sumner County Resource Authority has burned trash and garbage producing steam and a small amount of electricity. Other local industries purchase the steam and TVA purchases and distributes the electricity.

Three other distinct and separate developments since 1950 have contributed greatly to the quality of life enjoyed by Gallatin people. Old Hickory Lake, a vast reservoir formed by building a high dam on the Cumberland River at Old Hickory, put boating and aquatic sports of many kinds within easy reach. Men and women fishing from boats and banks swarmed the lake and found plenty of reason to return again and again. With the lake came a navigation channel deep enough for large commercial barge traffic and water enough to supply the cooling needs of the TVA Fossil Plant.

Construction of the bridge at Woods Ferry in the early 1950s provided the first all-season means of crossing the Cumberland from Gallatin for auto and truck traffic.

The bridge made possible the extension of State Highway 109 from the city to U.S. 70 and later to Interstate 40, the principal federal route in Tennessee as it passed through Wilson County.

Nothing was more beneficial to the education and general welfare of our people than the arrival of Volunteer State Community College in 1971. Since opening, it has become the benchmark by which the other state community colleges are measured. In the process, it has prepared local people of all ages for new careers and/or further education. It has offered a rich smorgasbord of learning opportunities.

Local history buffs convinced the mayor and council in 1993 that the city should own at least one historic site and with the assistance of a citizens' organization, make it available to the public. With two-thirds of the funds coming from the Rose Mont Restoration Foundation, Inc., the city acquired Rose Mont, the antebellum home of Catherine Blackmore (1806–1888) and Josephus Conn Guild (1802–1883). Theirs was one of Gallatin's all-time outstanding families. The foundation manages the site with volunteers, and rents the house for weddings, receptions, and meetings of various kinds. It oversees ongoing restoration using monies that it raises at the annual Rose Mont Renaissance and funds allotted by the city. The Gallatin Park System assists with lawn care and in other helpful ways.

Since the early 1950s, the appearance of Gallatin has changed dramatically. Although several old landmarks still stand, many others have fallen to the wrecker's ball. Handsome homes like Langley Hall on Coles Ferry Road, the George W. Allen house on East Franklin Street, and Barrymore on West Main Street were among the first. The John Bell Brown residence on Nashville Pike, the Dulin place built by Dr. H. A. Schell circa 1875 at the corner of Winchester and South Water Streets, and on North Water Street Dr. L. M. Woodson's Maple Valley and Frank Albright's home soon followed. And then there were the Octagon House on East Franklin, a two-story brick town house just east of the City Hall on West Main demolished in 1974, and Guildwood, an ornate Queen Anne-style house across the road from Rose Mont.

Changes in business and commerce have made a difference in the appearance of the city. In 1950 there were six or seven sprawling burley tobacco sales warehouses but only one in 2001. The number of lumber and building supply dealers has dwindled from five to one, the number of coal yards from three to none, and the number of independent pharmacies from six to one. Proprietary small hospitals and clinics, owned and operated by local medical doctors, have given way to a single public hospital, and a notorious 1940s slum area between Red River Road and West Eastland east of the railroad known as Muddy Run has been converted to productive use with the assistance of federal redevelopment project funds.

Widening the Nashville Pike from two lanes of traffic to five has changed the landscape along that entrance to town as has the similar widening of the Hartsville Pike in the eastern sector. Although it has reduced the traffic load on downtown streets, construction of the Highway 109 Bypass around the west side has further cut up long established vistas.

Two of the most obvious changes along East Main Street have been the elimination of Genesco's shoe manufacturing plant just east of the Public Square, and one hundred yards beyond, the demolition of Howard Elementary School on the site of old Howard College. Gallatin High School on the old Hawkins Preparatory School property met the same fate. Commercial development along East Main has resulted in the leveling of at least twenty-five houses that were standing in 1950. Similar changes have occurred along West Main, North and South Water Streets, and along West Eastland where even the L&N Railroad station house of 1860 was razed.

The Public Square of 2002 is much the same as it appeared in 1950. Many of the property owners have

Courtesy of Gallatin Chamber of Commerce
Volunteer State Community College.

restored and/or remodeled their buildings, but the structures remain intact. In cooperation with the Chamber of Commerce, the nonprofit organization Greater Gallatin, Inc., has taken the leading role in maintaining a viable downtown. Intervening rows of stores and offices seem securely anchored to the imposing corners such as the Guthrie Building, the First and Peoples National Bank Building, the Schamberger Building, and the buildings on the east and west side of South Water at its intersection with Main Street. A missing landmark of the 1950s, the city water tank that stood tall on long legs behind the west side of the square is gone, no longer hovering over the downtown with its painted-on greeting, "Welcome to Gallatin."

A significant number of plants opened by manufacturers who poured hundreds of millions of payroll dollars into the local economy during the last half of the twentieth century are no longer in operation. The demise of the local plants of Yale and Towne, the Shaffer Company, Hamilton-Cosco, Genesco, Globe Furniture, the Gary Company, Gallatin Aluminum Products Company, and others suggests that public support for economic development is an ongoing need. In these changing times, it is widely recognized that an effective, sustained effort is required to maintain and expand desirable levels of employment.

Large parking lots, products of the automotive age, punctuate the cityscape and sometimes threaten to absorb it, but we cannot do without them. Where would we park to attend a football game, to shop, to attend school or church, to visit the hospital, to go to work, to eat, or for the myriad other stops we make anytime we choose?

Gallatin currently shares the regrettable sameness that has overtaken towns and cities from coast to coast as national and regional retailers, restaurants, pharmacies, motels, gasoline stations, and other businesses usually move in with predetermined building designs. Appearances that distinguish one town from another are lost in the near uniformity of architectural shape, color, and presentation. Even certain public school buildings have lost their architectural distinctiveness with exterior facades that suggest they might be neat all-purpose warehouses. All of this is an interesting challenge to face.

The flow of people into and out of Gallatin on a daily basis is noteworthy. On school days, buses begin

By Walter T. Durham
Entrance sign at Sumner Regional Medical Center.

early in the morning bringing students to the schools in town. Industrial workers arrive about the same time. Among them are men and women from Westmoreland, Portland, Hendersonville, and Lebanon, often meeting Gallatin residents motoring to work in one of those towns in a strange exchange of the age. Commuting to work in Nashville has been a practice for a significant number of Gallatin people since the early 1900s when they traveled by train and/or the electric trolley called the Interurban. Since the 1930s commuting has been primarily by bus and auto. The new development since the 1950s has been the number of Nashvillians who commute to work in Gallatin. The college, the medical center, and attractive industrial employment have enticed many to work in the small city and retreat to Metro for time at home.

Throughout the day but mostly in the late afternoon, students and workers return home while late shift workers and others attending evening classes at the college flow into town. Whether inbound or outbound, commuting is an important part of life on the local scene.

Irrespective of its origins, the busy stop-and-go traffic on our streets and highways is symbolic of a people rarely at rest and a town trying to deal with the dynamics of change. What we do here during the years immediately ahead could set the tone for the rest of this century. In this free society, we face fabulous opportunities.

CHAPTER TWO

The Inner Workings

The charter of the city of Gallatin vests most authority to govern in the hands of the seven aldermen who together sit as the City Council. It is their responsibility to make policy and, in most cases, theirs to see that it is carried out.

The mayor is elected by popular vote for a term of four years. Although the power of the office is limited, the mayor can use it as a "bully pulpit" to keep important issues before the public and the council. He/she presides over council meetings, can freely express an opinion in all matters, but has no vote except in the election of certain city officials and whenever a tie occurs. At that point he/she can be a tiebreaker. The mayor also has veto power and can veto any action taken by the council provided that he/she does so within two whole days, Sundays excluded, and notifies each alderman within the twenty-four hours following. The council can override the veto if at least five aldermen vote to do so at the next regularly scheduled meeting.

For many years the council set policy when in session, but exercised its management responsibilities through committees. For example, at one time management was carried out by three committees of aldermen: Public Service, Public Safety, and Finance. More recently the aldermen handle management responsibilities and policy studies by meeting as a committee of the whole in work sessions. This method has the advantage of keeping all matters before the entire group thus minimizing the potential for misunderstandings or rivalry between committees.

Aldermen are elected by popular vote for four-year terms. Two are elected at large, but five are elected from as many aldermanic districts within the city. The purpose of election by district is to be certain that all areas of the city have representation in the council. The reason for electing at-large representatives is to have aldermen charged with seeing the big picture—that is, standing for what is best for the city as a whole versus the claims of specific districts. The council elects the mayor pro tem, usually referred to as vice mayor, from its own membership. The vice mayor acts when the mayor is absent or otherwise unable to fulfill the duties of office.

The charter makes provision for legal counsel. Elected by the council, the city attorney oversees the preparation of new ordinances and advises city officials on the interpretation and enforcement of existing laws. Although never domiciled in the City Hall, the office is vital to the functioning of city government.

Actual day-to-day management and supervision of most of the workings of government are accomplished by the heads of the six departments and four divisions. The department heads are the chief of police, the fire chief, the director of leisure services, the director of finance, the superintendent of public utilities, and the superintendent of public works. The city engineer, the city planner, the director of personnel, and the building official lead key divisions. An executive director manages the Economic Development Agency, and the Long Hollow Golf Course is supervised by a club professional and a course superintendent. A general manager oversees the department of electricity whose board members are appointed by the City Council.

The city recorder, elected every four years by popular vote, supervises the functions of that office which are primarily concerned with the collection of taxes and certain licensing matters. The recorder also functions as judge of the city traffic court which was started as a traffic court but now has jurisdiction to hear violations of all city ordinances.

What do the recorder and aldermen serving in 2001 think of Gallatin and its future? The general tenor of their responses to this question is positive and optimistic. Here are their comments:

Connie Kittrell, Recorder and City Judge—Like the rest of city government during the past twenty-five years, the office of the Recorder and City Judge has undertaken additional responsibilities. Almost all have been directly related to the growth of Gallatin.

This office has a ringside seat for observing Gallatin on the move because more business in town means more activity in our office. We see the increases in residential and commercial construction as we collect city property taxes. The installation of computers with the latest programs for real estate taxes and business licenses enables the office to be current in dealing with these matters and to serve increased loads in the future.

From the earliest days of Gallatin, the recorder has maintained the official records of the city. For better preservation and access, we expect soon to use electronic automation as we have in other areas.

As city judge, the recorder deals with traffic and code violations and issues related to planning and zoning. An increased docket reminds us that there are more of us in town and that growth continues.

Dr. J. Deotha Malone, Vice Mayor—As a career educator in the Sumner County School System, I am proud of Gallatin for the good environment in the city for public schools. Although there is a continuing need for more parental involvement with the schools and with their student children, the people of Gallatin have always held education in high regard. I have been impressed by the growing number of scholarships awarded at Gallatin Senior High School funded by local persons, businesses, churches, and others. Gallatin also generously supports scholarship programs at Volunteer State Community College. Everyone who cherishes success in education is greatly reassured by the accomplishments of Gallatin Senior High School graduates at both public and private institutions of higher learning where high academic standards prevail.

My sincere hope for the future is that all of us in city government and outside will do all that we can to maintain a positive environment for learning. There was a time one

By Allen Haynes

Police Department.

GALLATIN 200

Connie Kittrell.   *Dr. J. Deotha Malone.*   *John Alexander.*   *Craig Hayes.*

hundred years ago when a person could make a living, support a family, and have an acceptable quality of life without having received much schooling. Those days are gone forever. It is almost impossible to do the most menial of tasks today without being able to read and having some elementary knowledge of technology. Today's work force must be educated, and it is up to us to cultivate even broader public support for students and teachers and the schools where they study and teach.

John Alexander, Alderman—As an alderman and an employee of one of our largest industries, I can see how important the city is to industry and how important industry is to the city. I think this relationship will continue in the future. As other employers come to town, they will need a local government that can respond to their needs. I am not talking about giving away big bundles of money. What we must do is be prepared to extend the services that are normally expected of a city of our size. I think that our service departments are in good hands and can, with the help of the mayor and council, meet the needs of the future. In the meantime, we should monitor our relationships with current industries to be sure we know their needs.

Craig Hayes, Alderman—The importance of elected officials and the duty of voters to elect responsible candidates are only two of many things my politically active father has drummed into me. From my time as a member of the City Council, I have seen how important it is for the city to have dedicated persons making policy decisions. I see, too, how important it is for a councilperson to be supported by the voters when he or she faces tough decisions. It is equally urgent for officials to communicate with the public, to share information and perspectives so that we can understand each other even though we cannot always agree. Each of us represents voters, and we must reconcile individual voters' wishes with what we see as best for all of us.

Daryl Holt, Alderman—I really believe in the future of our city. After my college days, I came back home and went into business, a sure way to sink roots deep into any community. As an alderman, I see Gallatin for not only what it is, but for what it can be. The good life can be a better life especially if we all try to see that there are job and career opportunities for our young people. Our goal should be that upon graduation from high school or college, our children can feel confident of their futures when making a commitment to stay in Gallatin.

Robert Lea, Alderman—When I think about the future of Gallatin, I think about the town growing and its need for municipal services. We are blessed by having water supplied from a reservoir lake and electricity supplied from a local TVA plant. Those will be more than an adequate supply, but we will probably have to expand our delivery systems for both. We want to take every opportunity to assure that natural gas will be comparably available and distributed. Growth will strain sanitation

A Time Line History Celebrating the Bicentennial of Gallatin, Tennessee

By Allen Haynes
Daryl Holt.

By Walter Durham
Robert Lea.

By Allen Haynes
Ed Mayberry.

By Allen Haynes
Paul Perry.

services, but we have good sewage disposal facilities and burn our trash and garbage at the Sumner Resource Authority plant. I am sure the city will meet the needs of its citizens, but I want to be sure we are aware of how we stand in all service areas and have plans to meet future needs.

Ed Mayberry, Alderman—As I look to the future, I am reminded of how important it is for the city, like any individual or business, to have its finances in order. The city of Gallatin enjoys a good credit rating which means we receive extremely favorable interest rates when we borrow money for improvements. The city does not borrow money to fund operations but borrows by issuing bonds for such things as extending sewer, water, or gas lines, constructing a sewage disposal plant, and other capital-type developments. We face the job of reconciling fiscal restraint with meeting the community's legitimate needs. At the moment all is well. For the years ahead, we have to be alert to changes in the revenue stream, especially in revenues collected for us by the state of Tennessee. And we must be careful to finance the growth we face in a prudent, conservative way.

Paul Perry, Alderman—There's no question in my mind about future growth for Gallatin. Just look down the Nashville and Long Hollow Pikes, and you see it coming. Undoubtedly, this will bring tremendous opportunities for businesses and city offices as well. Like the business community, the city must be ready to adjust its services as needed. This is an exciting time, and by working together, we can make it a productive time for all. How very privileged we are to be a part of this awesome expansion in Gallatin!

Courtesy of Sumner County Museum

This 1923 Christmas greeting is from the family of the cartoonist, Dr. W. N. Lackey of Gallatin. The candle 1924 signifies the bright prospect of peace and good things in the approaching year. The rabbit represents Mayor-elect E. B. "Rabbit" House, now tied to City Hall, who had just defeated the incumbent W. H. Brown shown snuffing out the year 1923. The Courthouse of 1837 is pictured and labeled "same one" because Lackey wanted it replaced with a new one. The ladder-back chair memorializes the first Gallatin Mayor William Hadley, elected in 1822. Beneath the chair is a jar of moonshine whiskey, a pair of boots to be filled, and a bootjack. The "old board" of aldermen has been axed. "Old Gallatin" is shocked by how much the younger folks expect from Santa Claus. "Son citizen" is eager for new things, and the daughter is thinking of having an auto like her father's. Police Chief Bert Wallace holds his "billy" at the ready. The seven "aldermen" of the "New Board" are listed by profession: lawyer, pharmacist, tobacconist, carpenter, farmer, plumber, and insurance agent. The stockings hung from the mantel show that young Gallatin wants Santa to bring not only new streets but a filtration plant so that there will be plenty of pure water. The 1924 Almanac dangles from a corner of the mantel.

CHAPTER THREE

The Voters' Choice

Elected officials with broad ranges of backgrounds and experiences have served the city in leadership capacities from the earliest times. The five commissioners appointed by the legislature in 1801 to acquire the site for the county seat, subdivide it, and sell lots at public auction were landowners who realized the importance of local government. James "Curly" Wilson had already been captain in the county militia and had held the county office of straymaster. He had served as one of the eleven county seat location commissioners appointed in 1797 who could not reach a decision, and again as one of the third set of five commissioners in 1799 who were equally unable to agree. Appointed to the fourth and final set of commissioners in 1801, he must have had reason to celebrate when that group agreed on the site of Gallatin.

Another of the commissioners of 1801 was Samuel Donelson, a brother of Andrew Jackson's wife, Rachel, and a law partner of Jackson. He was a son of John Donelson who, with James Robertson, brought the first settlement parties to Middle Tennessee. The third was Charles Donoho, who had been a commissioner for the projected but never established town of Bledsoeborough on the Cumberland River between Dry Creek and Dixon's Creek. He was an attorney. Thomas Murray, the fourth, was a major in the county militia, and little is known about Shadrack Nye, the fifth, except that he was one of eighteen citizens who petitioned the legislature unsuccessfully in 1803 for an independent company of infantry for the town.

By the first of June 1804, the commissioners had fulfilled their duties and submitted a memo of expenses in the amount of $351.25. The Sumner County Court paid their expenses and relieved them of further duties.

As the courthouse and jail had been built by that time, the presence of the sheriff and other county officials and acts of the county court probably supplied such local government as was required. But recognizing the need to establish a government specifically for the town, the legislature created it by forming a council of five governing commissioners in 1806. Each was to be elected by popular vote for a two-year term. From their numbers they were to elect a chairman who would appoint a clerk and treasurer. This act provided for the first tax levy on citizens for town purposes and included maximum rates as follows: each town lot not to exceed fifty cents, each taxable white poll not over twelve and one half cents, and each taxable slave not over twenty-five cents. As no trace of local records of that time has survived, nothing is known of the identities of these commissioners or of their conduct of public affairs. Missing, also, are tax lists and any other information about the administration of the tax act.

In 1815 the legislature granted Gallatin a charter of incorporation. Two years later, the same body reorganized town government by abolishing the offices of commissioner and providing for the popular election of a mayor and seven aldermen. This basic form of municipal authority has continued through the city's two hundredth birthday, interrupted only from 1862 through 1864 and into 1865, the Civil War years of Union Army occupation. From 1831 to 1857, the mayor served, also, as one of the seven aldermen.

GALLATIN 200

Voters have chosen mayors and aldermen from the ranks of lawyers, doctors, dentists, retail merchants, wholesale distributors, manufacturers, educators, militia and state guard, bankers, industrial workers, skilled tradesmen, machine shop operators, insurance agents, warehousemen, realtors, investors, housewives, retirees, and almost any category imaginable. The characteristics held in common by all of the elected officials are their interest in undertaking the responsibility of public office and the public's confidence in them. By and large, the confidence of the voters seems to have been well placed.

Although most records kept by city officials prior to 1831 have not been preserved, a review of the names of known elected officials since that time can be rewarding. Partial compilations of such names have been made by city attorneys on three separate occasions, 1888, 1911, and 1929.

To bring the list current, City Recorder Connie Kittrell and her staff have researched the minutes of the City Council from 1855 to the present. The tedious task provides an accurate listing for the past 147 years.

Bound minutes of the City Council for the years 1831–1842 are preserved in a single volume in the manuscript section of the Sumner County Archives. The collection supplies the names of elected officials for that period.

The compilation of City Attorney Sumner A. Wilson published in 1888 reports the names of the mayor and city recorder of 1822, but of no other officials prior to 1831. Wilson wrote, and two more recent city attorneys researching the list have agreed, "The records of the corporation, embracing the period anterior to 1822 and down to 1831, being lost or not in existence, the list of authorities for the years between those dates is necessarily imperfect." In fact, the only names of city officials elected at any time prior to 1831 are those of the mayor and recorder of 1822. For the period from 1843–1854, Wilson's research is the only source of information now available.

The known stewards of the government of the city of Gallatin are listed below. Though sometimes inconsistent, the spelling and/or abbreviation of their names is as it appears in available records. When names are separated by a slash (/), it indicates that the first mentioned was succeeded by the next.

Civic Center.

By Allen Haynes

A Time Line History Celebrating the Bicentennial of Gallatin, Tennessee

Courtesy of Kenneth C. Thomson Jr. Collection
S. R. Anderson.

Courtesy of Kenneth C. Thomson Jr. Collection
William M. Blackmore.

Courtesy of Tennessee Historical Society
Thomas Boyers.

Courtesy of Walter T. Durham Collection
James Peacock.

1822—William Hadley, mayor; D. Fulton, recorder.

1831—James A. Blackmore, mayor; F. Chenault, recorder.
Aldermen: James L. McKoin, William Trousdale, Robert M. Boyers, James A. Blackmore, Daniel Saffarrans, John J. White.

1832—James L. McKoin, mayor; F. Chenault, recorder.
Aldermen: William Trousdale, James A. Blackmore, James L. McKoin, John Bell, John J. White, William Prince, F. Chenault.

1833—Daniel Saffarrans, mayor; F. Chenault, recorder.
Aldermen: William Trousdale, B. F. Simpson, Daniel Saffarrans, John Bell, R. M. Boyers, F. Chenault, John J. White.

1834—James L. McKoin, mayor; B. Watkins, recorder.
Aldermen: James A. Blackmore, James L. McKoin, Joseph C. Guild, William Trousdale, S. M. Blythe, R. M. Boyers, A. D. Bugg.

1835—James L. McKoin, mayor; B. Watkins, recorder.
Aldermen: R. M. Boyers, Daniel Saffarrans, J. L. McKoin, James A. Blackmore, Nat Prince, A. D. Bugg, John J. White.

1836—William M. Blackmore, mayor; B. Watkins, recorder.
Aldermen: James A. Blackmore, S. M. Blythe, W. M. Blackmore, Benjamin Gray, N. Prince, Jacob L. Warner, Robert G. Douglass.

1837—William M. Blackmore, mayor; B. Watkins, recorder.
Aldermen: James A. Blackmore, Benjamin Gray, W. M. Blackmore, S. M. Blythe, R. G. Douglass, Charles Lewis, J. R. A. Tomkins.

1838—William M. Blackmore, mayor; B. Watkins, recorder and treasurer.
Aldermen: W. M. Blackmore, Jo. C. Guild, William Solomon, R. G. Douglass, J. L. Warner, Benjamin R. Howard, Samuel F. Schell.

1839—William M. Blackmore, mayor; B. Watkins, recorder and treasurer.
Aldermen: George Love, R. M. Boyers, W. P. Rowles, W. M. Blackmore, S. R. Anderson, Jo C. Guild, Charles G. Sanders.

1840—William Solomon, mayor; B. Watkins, recorder and treasurer.
Aldermen: S. R. Anderson, H. B. Vaughan, William Solomon, S. T. Schell, Benjamin Edwards, J. R. A. Tomkins, Jo. C. Guild.

1841—Samuel R. Anderson, mayor; B. Watkins, recorder and treasurer.
Aldermen: W. M. Blackmore, Jo. C. Guild, William Solomon, S. R. Anderson, James Alexander, Francis Youree, George Love.

1842—Oscar Staley, mayor; B. Watkins, recorder and treasurer.
Aldermen: George Love, Francis Youree, James Alexander, William Trousdale, Oscar Staley, W. M. Blackmore, Charles Lewis.

1843—George Love, mayor; Reuben D. Green, recorder and treasurer.
Aldermen: George Love, William E. Elliott, Francis Youree, James Alexander, W. M. Brigg, W. M. Blackmore, Jo. C. Guild.

1844—George Love, mayor; Reuben D. Green, recorder and treasurer.
Aldermen: George Love, William Solomon, Francis Youree, S. R. Anderson, W. M. Blackmore, D. C. Gasskill, H. B. Vaughan.

1845—George F. Crockett, mayor; James Alexander, recorder and treasurer.

GALLATIN 200

Aldermen: James Alexander, William H. Edwards, George F. Crockett, George Love, John W. Franklin, Francis Youree, W. M. Blackmore.

1846—William Solomon, mayor; James Alexander, recorder and treasurer.

Aldermen: William H. Edwards, Francis Youree, John W. Franklin, William Solomon, William Moore, Z. W. Baker, James Alexander.

1847—William Solomon, mayor; James Alexander, recorder and treasurer.

Aldermen: William Solomon, William Moore, W. W. Thomas, B. R. Howard, Z. W. Baker, James Alexander, William M. Briggs.

1848—William M. Blackmore, mayor; James Alexander, recorder and treasurer.

Aldermen: H. J. Barker, William Moore, Z. W. Baker, W. M. Blackmore, W. W. Thomas, William Wright, James Alexander.

1849—William M. Blackmore, mayor; James Alexander, recorder and treasurer.

Aldermen: W. M. Blackmore, W. W. Thomas, H. J. Barker, Z. W. Baker, William Wright, W. C. Moore, James Alexander.

1850—William M. Blackmore, mayor; William Wright, recorder and treasurer.

Aldermen: W. M. Blackmore, C. B. King, H. T. George, W. W. Thomas, W. C. Moore, William Henley, William Wright.

1851—William M. Blackmore, mayor; William Wright, recorder and treasurer.

Aldermen: W. M. Blackmore, G. S. Gray, R. Williamson, W. C. Moore, William Wright, William Moore, W. W. Thomas.

1852—William M. Blackmore, mayor; William Wright, recorder and treasurer.

Aldermen: W. M. Blackmore, George Love, W. C. Moore, Alexander Barnes, R. Williamson, Joab Horn, G. S. Gray.

1853—George Love, mayor; William Wright, recorder and treasurer.

Aldermen: James S. Johnson, George Love, B. R. Howard, William Moore, William Wright, G. S. Gray, W. N. Montgomery.

1854—G. S. Gray, mayor; Daniel T. McKoin, recorder and treasurer.

Aldermen: James S. Johnson, Daniel T. McKoin, W. N. Montgomery, G. S. Gray, John H. Trigg, W. C. Moore, George Love.

1855—Thomas Boyers, mayor; John G. Turner, recorder and treasurer.

Aldermen: Robert Williamson, Joseph Natcher, William Wright, John H. Malone, William Solomon, G. S. Gray, Thomas Boyers.

1856—Thomas Boyers, mayor; John G. Turner, recorder and treasurer.

Aldermen: Robert Williamson, Joseph Natcher, William Wright, John H. Malone, William Solomon, G. S. Gray, Thomas Boyers.

1857—James S. Johnson, mayor; John G. Turner, recorder and treasurer.

Aldermen: William Wright, John H. Malone, John B. Foster, William Moore, William C. Knight, Joab Horn, W. C. Blue.

1858—John H. Trigg, mayor; John G. Turner, recorder and treasurer.

Aldermen: William Wright, John B. Foster, William C. Knight, Joab Horn, William Moore, John H. Malone, W. C. Blue.

1859—John H. Trigg, mayor; S. F. Schell, recorder and treasurer.

Aldermen: John B. Foster, Baxter Smith, W. C. Blue, W. C. Knight, William Wright, Joab Horn, D. P. Hart.

1860—John H. Trigg, mayor; S. F. Schell, recorder and treasurer.

Aldermen: John B. Foster, Baxter Smith, W. C. Blue, W. C. Knight, William Wright, Joab Horn, D. P. Hart.

1861—W. N. Montgomery, mayor, resigned; W. C. Knight, mayor, pro tem; S. F. Schell, recorder and treasurer.

Aldermen elect—W. C. Blue, John B. Foster, William Wright, W. C. Knight, F. D. Blackmore, Baxter Smith, D. P. Hart.

November 20, 1861, D. P. Hart, W. C. Blue, and Baxter Smith resigned, and A. M. Barber and H. J. Barker were elected to fill out two of the unexpired terms.

1862—James W. Johnson, mayor; S. F. Schell, recorder.

Aldermen: John B. Foster, F. A. Sporer, W. C. Knight, H. A. Schell, F. D. Blackmore, Jonas Nickelson, William Wright.

On January 4, 1862, the recorder entered the names of these officials in the minutes, but there were no other entries of any kind until the end of the war on April 28, 1865.

1865—James S. Johnson, mayor; S. F. Schell, recorder.

Aldermen: John B. Foster, F. A. Sporer, W. C. Knight, H. A. Schell, F. D. Blackmore, Jonas Nickelson, William Wright.

A Time Line History Celebrating the Bicentennial of Gallatin, Tennessee

1866—Robert Hallum, mayor; S. F. Schell, recorder.

Aldermen: H. P. Enlow, John B. Foster, W. C. Blue, William Moore, D. P. Hart, Jonas Nickelson, S. Hermans.

1867—Robert Hallum, mayor; S. Hermans, recorder.

Aldermen: John B. Foster, William Wright, William Moore, William H. Crump, Jonas Nickelson, H. P. Enlow, C. C. Cantrell.

1868—William Wright, mayor; S. Hermans, recorder.

Aldermen: William Moore, William Crump, John B. Foster, H. P. Enlow, C. C. Cantrell, Jonas Nickelson, William Wright.

The above officials held office until May 8, 1868, when they were superceded by the board elected under the act of December 3, 1867, under which I. N. Phillips, Commissioner of Registration, held the election. The new officers met May 8, 1868.

James Peacock, mayor; S. Hermans, recorder.

Aldermen: L. H. Alley, J. V. Minor, T. McKinley, J. H. Needles, I. N. Phillips, and freedmen Columbus Johnson and Willis Motley.

J. H. Needles and I. N. Phillips resigned as aldermen. H. P. Enlow and Charles Porter replaced them.

1869—James Peacock, mayor; H. C. McQuiddy, recorder.

Aldermen: T. McKinley, C. B. King/H. C. McQuiddy, Thomas Allison/Nelson Turner, J. V. Minor, J. F. Lauck, and two freedmen, H. W. Key and Houston Bowers.

After April 3, 1869, the above board recorded no meetings for the rest of the year.

1870—Isaac W. Harris, mayor; D. P. Hart, recorder.

Aldermen: Samuel Nicholson, B. F. Jemison, Miles B. Henley, James M. Whitesides, F. D. Blackmore, Robert Strother/John Clark, W. C. Blue.

1871—Isaac W. Harris, mayor; D. P. Hart, recorder.

Aldermen: Samuel Nicholson, B. F. Jemison/R. E. Moore, W. C. Blue, H. Tibbett, James M. Whitesides, W. B. Henley, F. D. Blackmore.

1872—W. S. Munday, mayor; Hy Crutcher/G. B. Wright/D. P. Hart/Polk Blakemore/W. H. Brown, recorder.

Aldermen: W. R. Tompkins, J. C. Rodemer, Thomas H. King, G. B. Wright, J. E. Howard, F. D. Blackmore, M. S. Elkins.

F. D. Blackmore resigned and C. W. Trousdale was elected. C. W. Trousdale and J. E. Howard resigned and James House and H. Tibbett were elected. H. Tibbett resigned and James A. Mentlo succeeded him.

W. S. Munday resigned as mayor and S. Hermans was elected. Hy Crutcher resigned as recorder to be followed by G. B. Wright, D. P. Hart, Polk Blakemore, and W. H. Brown.

As no local newspapers from 1872 are known to have survived and the Council Minutes recorded the resignations and elections without comment, there seems to be no explanation for the apparent confusion.

1873—Isaac W. Harris, mayor; W. H. Brown, recorder.

Aldermen: G. B. Wright, Samuel Nicholson, H. A. Schell, W. R. Tomkins, R. E. Moore, Thomas H. King, W. J. Henley.

1874—James M. Whitesides, mayor; William Clark, recorder.

Aldermen: Samuel Nicholson, H. A. Schell, W. C. Blue, Carroll Cocke, T. C. Buckingham, S. R. Simpson, D. McVaw.

1875—W. C. Blue, mayor; W. H. Brown, recorder.

Aldermen: James S. Tomkins, S. R. Simpson, W. R. Tomkins, D. B. Anderson, Samuel Nicholson, J. E. Howard, Thomas Buckingham.

1876—W. C. Blue, mayor; W. H. Brown, recorder.

Aldermen: Samuel R. Nicholson, T. L. Buckingham, W. R. Tomkins, D. B. Anderson, J. E. Howard, H. A. Schell, Carroll Cocke.

1877—W. C. Blue, mayor; W. H. Brown, recorder.

Aldermen: Samuel Nicholson, W. R. Tomkins, H. A. Schell, D. B. Anderson, J. E. Howard, Carroll Cocke, T. L. Buckingham.

1878—John B. Foster, mayor; W. H. Brown, recorder.

Aldermen: Carroll Cocke, T. L. Buckingham, James House, D. K. Spillers, W. J. Henley, H. A. Schell, D. P. Hart.

1879—John B. Foster, mayor; T. L. Buckingham, recorder.

Aldermen: W. R. Tomkins, D. K. Spillers, George N. Guthrie, B. F. Buckingham, John W. Walton, Carroll Cocke, T. J. Day.

1880—W. C. Blue, mayor; W. H. Brown, recorder.

Aldermen: George N. Guthrie, James House, W. R. Tomkins, T. M. Woodson, D. P. Hart, H. A. Schell, J. W. Brown.

1881—John B. Foster, mayor; W. H. Brown, recorder.
Aldermen: D. P. Hart, W. R. Tomkins, John Fry, W. C. Blue, W. G. Montgomery, T. M. Woodson, Carroll Cocke.

1882—John B. Foster, mayor; W. H. Brown, recorder.
Aldermen: H. H. DeWitt, L. H. Gray, D. H. Hart, Ernest Franklin, John Fry, Carroll Cocke, J. T. Walton.

1883—George N. Guthrie, mayor; John W. Knight, recorder.
Aldermen: J. T. Walton, I. W. Harris Jr., W. R. Tomkins, Samuel Lyon, W. C. Blue, T. H. King, H. A. Schell.

1884—George N. Guthrie, mayor; W. H. Brown, recorder.
Aldermen: Isaac Harris, Samuel Lyon, W. R. Tomkins, H. H. DeWitt, Carroll Cocke, John B. Foster, T. H. King.

1885—George N. Guthrie, mayor; W. H. Brown, recorder.
Aldermen: Isaac Harris, Samuel Lyon, W. R. Tomkins. H. H. DeWitt, Carroll Cocke, John B. Foster, J. T. Walton.

1886–1887—G. R. Dismukes, mayor; John W. Knight, recorder.
Aldermen: X. B. Haynie, W. R. Tomkins, H. H. DeWitt, John Fry, Samuel Lyon, J. T. Walton, Carroll Cocke.

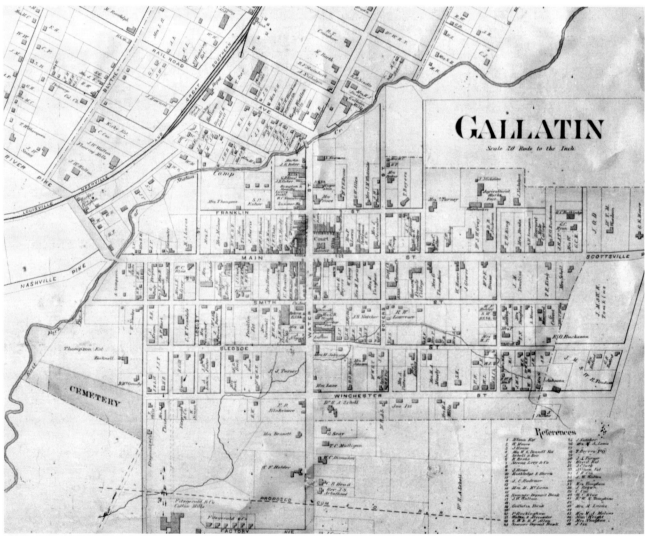

Gallatin map from Beers' 1878 map of Sumner County.

Courtesy of Tennessee State Library and Archives

A Time Line History Celebrating the Bicentennial of Gallatin, Tennessee

Courtesy of Kenneth C. Thomson Jr. Collection
George N. Guthrie.

Courtesy of Kenneth C. Thomson Jr. Collection
John B. Donelson.

Courtesy of Kenneth C. Thomson Jr. Collection
James W. Blackmore.

Courtesy of Kenneth C. Thomson Jr. Collection
W. G. Schamberger.

1888—George N. Guthrie, mayor; J. W. Ruswurm, recorder.
Aldermen: W. G. Schamberger, Samuel Lyon, John Fry, John M. Cantrell, D. K. Spillers, H. H. DeWitt, W. C. Blue.

1889—George N. Guthrie, mayor; J. W. Russwurm, recorder.
Aldermen: Samuel Lyon/A. E. House, H. H. DeWitt, W. G. Schamberger, J. M. Cantrell, W. C. Blue, John Fry, E. O. Buchanan.

1890–1891—George N. Guthrie, mayor; W. H. Joyner, recorder.
Aldermen: R. E. House, John Fry, J. M. Cantrell, T. S. Ellis, Carroll Cocke, E. O. Buchanan, W. H. Brown/S. F. Wilson.

1892–1893—George N. Guthrie, mayor; T. S. Vinson, recorder.
Aldermen: J. M. Cantrell, W. A. J. Simpson, W. F. Roth, B. E. Love, W. C. Blue/Dr. L. M. Woodson, Ernest Franklin, C. B. Brown.

1894–1895—George N. Guthrie, mayor; T. S. Vinson, recorder.
Aldermen: C. B. Brown, J. M. Cantrell, Ernest Franklin, W. M. Keen, W. F. Roth, W. A. J. Simpson/B. E. Love, Dr. L. M. Woodson.

1896–1897—J. B. Donelson, mayor; T. S. Vinson/J. O. Dillard/W. L. Oldham, recorder.
Aldermen: C. B. Brown, Ernest Franklin, W. F. Roth/W. C. Blue, A. R. Schell, George T. House, W. M. Keen, R. M. Jones.

1898–1899—J. B. Donelson, mayor; W. L. Oldham, recorder.
Aldermen: D. K. Spillers, E. O. Buchanan, B. E. Love, W. G. Schamberger, John Fry, R. M. Jones, A. R. Schell.

1900–1901—J. W. Blackmore, mayor; W. L. Oldham, recorder.
Aldermen: John Fry, Ernest Franklin, H. R. Fidler, R. E. House, C. B. Brown, Dr. L. M. Woodson, W. G. Schamberger.

1902–1903—James W. Blackmore, mayor; W. L. Oldham, recorder.
Aldermen: A. R. Schell, Ernest Franklin, C. B. Brown, Dr. L. M. Woodson, W. G. Schamberger, B. E. Love, R. E. House.

1904–1905—James W. Blackmore, mayor; W. L. Oldham, recorder.
Aldermen: Ernest Franklin, W. G. Schamberger, R. E. House, C. B. Brown, Dr. L. M. Woodson, B. E. Love, A. R. Schell.

1906–1907—James W. Blackmore, mayor; W. L. Oldham, recorder.
Aldermen: C. B. Brown, Ernest Franklin, J. R. Person, R. E. House, M. A. Ewing, J. J. Naive, J. E. Cron.

1908–1909—A. M. Blue, mayor; R. E. House, mayor pro tem; W. L. Oldham, recorder.
Aldermen: J. E. Cron, W. W. Pardue, J. J. Naive, M. A. Ewing, Ed L. Anderson, C. B. Brown, J. R. Person.

1910–1911—W. G. Schamberger, mayor; W. L. Oldham, recorder.
Aldermen: John Fry, B. A. Williams, Ed L. Anderson, W. W. Pardue, R. T. Ramsey/C. E. Powell, J. W. McCormick, J. C. O'Dell.

1912–1913—W. B. Brown, mayor; W. L. Oldham, recorder.
Aldermen: M. S. Elkins/Max R. Bandy, John Fry, B. H. Hix, Dr. Walter Dotson, T. J. Cook, W. W. Pardue, E. L. Anderson/Ernest Franklin.

1914–1915—W. B. Brown/John Fry, mayor; W. L. Oldham/H. Orman, recorder.

Gallatin 200

Former Mayors William P. Puryear, Ed McDonald, Cordell McDonald, and Ottis Kemp with Mayor Fred A. Kelly in background.

Courtesy of Sumner County Archives

Aldermen: John Fry/M. S. Elkin, W. H. Brown, W. N. Robertson, R. W. Caldwell, E. T. Jones, John Harris.

1916–1917—Harry A. Holder, mayor; H. Orman, recorder.

Aldermen: A. C. Earls, R. T. Guthrie, C. E. Hewgley/J. R. Person, Frank Seay, F. A. Woodward, John Harris/S. W. Williams, W. H. Brown.

1918–1919—Harry A. Holder, mayor; H. Orman, recorder.

Aldermen: W. H. Brown, R. T. Guthrie, B. H. Hix, J. R. Person, Frank Seay, S. W. Williams, F. A. Woodward.

1920–1921—W. H. Brown, mayor; H. Orman, recorder.

Aldermen: W. N. Robertson, J. H. Ewing, E. F. Hickman, R. T. Guthrie, Frank Seay, F. A. Woodward, J. R. Person.

1922–1923—W. H. Brown, mayor; E.E. Person, recorder.

Aldermen: J. H. Ewing, R. T. Guthrie, Frank Hunter, Sam E. Lackey, J. R. Person, Frank Seay, F.A. Woodward.

1924–1925—E. B. House, mayor; E. E. Person, recorder.

Aldermen: N. B. Echols, J. A. Harrison, J. L. Maddox, J. W. Murrey, C. E. Perkins/Max R. Bandy, W. A. J. Simpson, Lee Duke.

1926–1927—Max R. Bandy, mayor; E. E. Person, recorder.

Aldermen: George W. Allen, R. E. Cron, Horace E. Franklin, John C. Franklin, G. W. Mitchell, W. P. Warren, N. B. Echols.

1928–1929—Lee Duke, mayor; E. E. Person, recorder.

Aldermen: L. W. Hite, W. N. Robertson, H. E. Franklin, F. A. Kelly Jr., E. E. Turner, N. B. Echols, W. P. Warren.

1930–1931—George Mitchell, mayor; W. A. J. Simpson, recorder.

Aldermen: E. B. Craig, J. A. Christian, Fred Outlaw, T. L. Watkins, Perry A. West, Horace E. Franklin, L. W. Hite.

1932–1933—George Mitchell, mayor; W. A. J. Simpson, recorder.

Aldermen: John R. Harris, Norval S. Baker, Harold Hix, E. W. Thompson, Fred Outlaw, L. W. Hite, Horace E. Franklin.

1934–1935—L.W. Hite, mayor; W. A. J. Simpson, recorder.

Aldermen: Fred Outlaw, E. M. Stark, Avery Clark, Lee Duke, Harold Hix, Norval S. Baker, Horace E. Franklin.

1936–1937—L. W. Hite, mayor; W. A. J. Simpson/Lee Smith/H. H. Anderson, recorder.

Aldermen: Fred Outlaw, Lee Duke, Avery Clark, E. M. Stark, Harold Hix, Norval S. Baker, Horace E. Franklin.

1938–1939—A. N. Fuller, mayor; H. H. Anderson, recorder.

Aldermen: Horace E. Franklin, Fred Outlaw, Norval S. Baker, E. M. Stark, W. P. Puryear Jr., E. W. Thompson, Frank Seay.

1940–1941—A. N. Fuller/Horace E. Franklin, mayor; Dan Gaines, recorder.
Aldermen: Horace E. Franklin/H. H. Maddox, Fred Outlaw, Norval S. Baker, E. M. Stark, W. P. Puryear Jr., E. W. Thompson, Frank Seay.

1942–1943—W. P. Puryear Jr., mayor; Dan Gaines, recorder.
Aldermen: Fred Outlaw, Norval S. Baker, E. M. Stark, E. W. Thompson, Frank Seay, Ben Barry, Robert T. Guthrie.

1944–1945—W. P. Puryear Jr., mayor; Dan Gaines, recorder.
Aldermen: Ben Barry, Robert T. Guthrie, Fred Outlaw, Norval S. Baker, E. M. Stark, E. W. Thompson, Frank Seay.

1946–1947—W. P. Puryear Jr., mayor; R. L. Neal, recorder.
Aldermen: Fred Outlaw, Norval S. Baker, E. W. Thompson, Frank Seay, William McLean, Virgil Shaw, Robert T. Guthrie.

1948–1949—E. W. Thompson, mayor; R. L. Neal, recorder.
Aldermen: Norval S. Baker, Frank Seay, William McLean, O. M. Dalton, J. G. Bradley, W. T. Chandler, Robert T. Guthrie.

1950–1951—E. W. Thompson, mayor; I. C. Brown, recorder.
Aldermen: Robert Maddox, John Franklin, Joe St. Charles, I. C. Brown, O. M. Dalton, William McLean, Norval S. Baker.

1952–1953—E. W. Thompson, mayor; I. C. Brown, recorder.
Aldermen: J. C. Crutcher, Ottis Kemp, Rutledge Kittrell, I. C. Brown, Joe St. Charles, John Franklin, Robert Maddox.

1954–1955—E. W. Thompson, mayor; I. C. Brown, recorder.
Aldermen: Robert N. Durham, E. G. Mattox, John Franklin, Joe St. Charles, I. C. Brown, J. C. Crutcher, Ottis Kemp.

1956–1957—E. W. Thompson, mayor; I. C. Brown, recorder.
Aldermen: Robert N. Durham, E. G. Mattox, Rutledge Kittrell, Ottis Kemp, J. C. Crutcher/Ed McDonald, I. C. Brown, Joe St. Charles.

1958–1959—E. W. Thompson, mayor; I. C. Brown, recorder.
Aldermen: Fount Lyles, Felix Fly, John Franklin, Joe St. Charles, I. C. Brown, Ottis Kemp, E. G. Mattox.

1960–1961—E. W. Thompson, mayor; I. C. Brown, recorder.
Aldermen: Fount Lyles, Felix Fly, Ed McDonald, James Ditty, A. W. Harpole, Ottis Kemp, John Franklin.

Courtesy of Crutcher Studio

City Hall Annex, City Hall and Fire Department, Police Station, and Department of Electricity, c. 1960.

Gallatin 200

Courtesy of Sumner County Archives
Fred A. Kelly.

Courtesy of Sumner County Archives
Byron Charlton.

By Allen Haynes
John Hancock.

Courtesy of Sumner County Archives
David Schreiner.

1962–1963—Ed McDonald, mayor; W. T. Donoho, recorder.
Aldermen: Monroe Brooks, Bill Caruthers, Cortez Ford, Townes B. Johnson, Bettye Scott, James Ditty, Ottis Kemp.

1964–1965—Ed McDonald/Ottis Kemp, mayor; W. T. Donoho, recorder.
Aldermen: Monroe Brooks, Bill Caruthers, Cortez Ford, Townes B. Johnson, Bettye Scott/Dr. Hal Hooper, Jimmy Ditty, Ottis Kemp.

1966–1967—Ottis Kemp, mayor; W. T. Donoho, recorder.
Aldermen: James Ditty, Cortez Ford, Bettye Scott, Dr. Hal Hooper, I. C. Brown, Paul Enoch, Jack Kittrell.

1968–1969—Ottis Kemp, mayor; W. T. Donoho, recorder.
Aldermen: James Ditty, Bettye Scott, Dr. Hal Hooper, I. C. Brown, Paul Enoch, Jack Kittrell, Howard Maddox.

1970–1971—Cordell McDonald, mayor; W. T. Donoho, recorder.
Aldermen: James Ditty, Richard Fenker, J. Deotha Malone, J. O. Templeton, Thomas Suddarth, Howard Maddox, Jack Kittrell.

1972–1973—Cordell McDonald, mayor; W. T. Donoho, recorder.
Aldermen: J. Deotha Malone, Richard Fenker, J. O. Templeton, Thomas Suddarth, Fred A. Kelly, Jerry Metcalf, Joe Womack.

1974–1975—Fred A. Kelly, mayor; W. T. Donoho, recorder.
Aldermen: J. Deotha Malone, Byron Charlton, E. G. Mattox, Joe Womack, Jerry Metcalf, Richard Fenker, J. O. Templeton.

1976–1977—Fred A. Kelly, mayor; W. T. Donoho/ Peggy Harris, recorder.

Courtesy of Sumner County Archives
Dick Dempsey.

Courtesy of Sumner County Archives
Tommy Garrott.

Courtesy of Sumner County Archives
Robert W. Lankford.

A Time Line History Celebrating the Bicentennial of Gallatin, Tennessee

Aldermen: J. Deotha Malone, Richard Fenker, J. O. Templeton, Joe Womack, Byron Charlton, E. G. Mattox, Henry Frank Ferrell.

1978–1979—Byron Charlton, mayor; Frank Shaw, recorder.

Aldermen: J. Deotha Malone, Russ Melvin, Robert Neal Durham, Harold Smith, Henry Frank Ferrell, J. O. Templeton, Richard Fenker.

1980–1981—Byron Charlton, mayor; Frank Shaw, recorder.

Aldermen: Richard Fenker, J. Deotha Malone, J. O. Templeton, Russ Melvin, Harold Smith, Randy Hampton, Steve Canter.

1982–1983—John Hancock, mayor; Robert W. Lankford, recorder.

Aldermen: J. Deotha Malone, Bruce Kittrell, Anne Kemp, David Schreiner, Randy Hampton, Steve Canter, Harold Smith.

1984–1985—John Hancock, mayor; Robert W. Lankford, recorder.

Aldermen: J. Deotha Malone, Randy Hampton, Bruce Kittrell, Anne Kemp, David Schreiner, Byron Charlton/Jim Hunter, Harold Smith.

1986–1987—David Schreiner, mayor; Robert W. Lankford, recorder.

Aldermen: J. Deotha Malone, Harold Smith, Randy Hampton, Bruce Kittrell, Tommy Garrott, Jim Womack, Bettye Scott.

1988–1989—David Schreiner, mayor; Robert W. Lankford, recorder.

Aldermen: J. Deotha Malone, Bruce Kittrell, Tommy Garrott, Dick Dempsey, John Hancock, Bettye Scott, Jim Womack.

1990–1991—David Schreiner/Dick Dempsey, mayor; Robert W. Lankford, recorder.

Aldermen: J. Deotha Malone, John Hancock, Tommy Garrott, Bettye Scott, Anne Kemp, Angela Wallace, Dick Dempsey.

1992–1993—Tommy Garrott, mayor; Robert W. Lankford, recorder.

Aldermen: J. Deotha Malone, Baker Ring, Harold Jackson, Bobby Shults, Ed Mayberry, Anne Kemp, Angela Wallace.

1994–1995—Robert W. Lankford, mayor; Connie W. Kittrell, recorder.

Aldermen: J. Deotha Malone, Jo Ann Graves, William Rogan, Yvonne Malone, Ed Mayberry, Bobby Shults, Baker Ring.

1996–1997—Robert W. Lankford, mayor; Connie W. Kittrell, recorder.

Aldermen: J. Deotha Malone, William Rogan, John Ruth, David Black, Phyllis Hovenden, John Alexander, Ed Mayberry.

1998–1999—Don Wright, mayor; Connie W. Kittrell, recorder.

Aldermen: J. Deotha Malone, Robert Lea, Ed Mayberry, John Alexander, Craig Hayes, Daryl Holt, John Ruth.

2000–2001—Don Wright, mayor; Connie W. Kittrell, recorder.

Aldermen: J. Deotha Malone, Daryl Holt, Craig Hayes, John Alexander, Ed Mayberry, Robert Lea, Wayne Brooks/Paul Perry.

Part Two

CHAPTER FOUR

Time Line History

GALLATIN 1802–2002

An accurate chronology of events is essential to understanding history at any level. The order of things alone can answer many questions. With knowledge of that progression, the assessment of cause and effect can be much more reliable. Without that determination, we would face a past that offers only very limited guidance for the future.

The following pages present a time line history of Gallatin, Tennessee, a listing of selected events that have influenced its growth, and the quality of life its citizens share. The focus is intentionally narrow, but occasional mention is made of national and international happenings. For the most part, the files of local newspapers and the minutes of the Board of Aldermen, now usually called the City Council, have provided most of the information for this undertaking. Investigation has extended to Nashville newspapers, books, magazines, journals, manuscripts, documents, county and state records, and other sources. Nonetheless, obvious gaps appear in the chronology where research has been unproductive.

Perhaps the most difficult story to capture in a recitation of this kind was the institution of slavery, its practice, and its final abolition in 1865. Comparably challenging is the life and culture of African Americans no longer slaves but socially and economically segregated for the next ninety-nine years.

The integration of schools and public facilities in response to the Civil Rights Act of 1964 changed local racial customs and practices more than one hundred years old. There was no longer a legal basis for separating students or workers or friends because of race.

A time line cannot report adequately the many social services that are delivered by churches, fraternal orders, civic clubs, patriotic organizations, independent charities, and other not-for-profit groups. The range of services extends from eye care to housing for the elderly and includes food and clothing for the indigent, a safe haven for victims of domestic violence, Habitat for Humanity houses, and much more. Even excluding the greater part of social services provided by local, state, and federal governments, there could be an entire book written about the private sector's contributions.

It is difficult also in this format to share the experiences of individual persons. Throughout two centuries of wars, many local men and women have been selfless heroes. The sacrifices of some have extended even to giving their own lives. Also of great importance are the contributions so many have made during times of peace to sustain and improve the community in which they have lived. Behind and in the middle of every event chronicled are real, live persons whose stories need telling but, alas, not within the limits space imposes.

Because it is event centered, the time line rarely mentions persons, but there are necessary exceptions to this practice. One is mentioning the name of the author of the first book published in Gallatin. The many writers since his period of the early 1800s are largely ignored, but if they have written about local history in magazines or books, most of their names appear in the bibliography of this volume. The chronology identifies general officers in the military, elected United States senators and representatives, governors, and certain other outstanding public figures of larger than local dimension.

Due to the growth of the town and region since World War I, twentieth-century developments receive what might appear to be a disproportionately large amount of attention. But the change from a farming town to a community that embraced industry, a college, racial desegregation, the newly impounded waters of Old Hickory Lake, and a regional medical center requires acknowledgment.

Significant industrial development characterized the twentieth century, and as it broadly affected the economic welfare of the citizenry, it receives prominent and frequent mention. The needs of education, suggested by a grand increase in school building construction, generated public interest and support during the same period. The opening of Volunteer State Community College nearly three decades ago and the extension of its services throughout the region have been a source of pride to local people, especially those who had long coveted an institution of higher learning for Gallatin.

Though hardly fifty years old, Old Hickory Lake has become a remarkable resource. Its shoreline has supplied thousands of home sites and numerous locations for boat docks and public access areas.

One of the most important developments of the last half-century has been the increasing role of Sumner Regional Medical Center in the delivery of medical services to the north central region of Middle Tennessee. Any discussion of Gallatin during the last fifty years must include frequent mention of the hospital, its growth, and its outreach.

This chronology includes little about churches after noting the organization of the first few and the construction of some of the principal houses of worship. This conscious omission is to be more than offset by another bicentennial project: the compilation of local church histories by individual congregations. The celebration committee will gather the narratives and include them in a special Gallatin 200 file in the Sumner County Archives where they will be freely available to researchers.

The existence of numerous civic clubs, fraternal orders, and other such organizations receive the barest minimum of coverage, but again, this is a time for the members of each to compile its history. These will, in turn, be deposited in a special file at the Sumner Archives.

But let the story now unfold. It all began on a spread of undeveloped land in a sixteen-year-old county where a town was started literally from the ground up. The following time line lists events in the years in which they occurred; in the years in which more than a single event is mentioned, the listings are generally in the order of occurrence. The last entry was made on October 11, 2001, four days before taking the book to press. Photographs and sidebars illustrate and elaborate many of the entries.

GALLATIN 200

1801 The General Assembly appoints five Sumner County Commissioners to select site for county seat town to be called Gallatin.

1802 Town is created when commissioners select and purchase site, lay out town lots, and sell them at auction. • Andrew Jackson purchases one of the lots that, around 1974, became a part of the City Hall property on West Main Street. • General James Winchester completes construction of Cragfont, then the grandest house on the Tennessee frontier.

1803 Builders complete construction of county courthouse, jail, and stocks. • Andrew Jackson and John Hutchings open general store on lot Jackson purchased the prior year.

By Allen Haynes

Walnut Grove built circa 1795 just west of the future site of Gallatin.

1804 Thomas Jefferson re-elected president of the United States. • Gallatin hosts first local horse races over a public track.

1806 General Assembly establishes council of five commissioners to govern the town. • Charter is issued for Transmontania Academy.

1807 First book by local author is published: *Clark's Miscellany in Prose and Verse* by Isaac Clark.

1808 King Solomon Lodge of F.&A.M., No. 6 in the state, receives charter.

1809 Town annexes twenty-nine acres of land on east side.

1812 Congress declares war on Great Britain. • Volunteers organize local companies for military duty with General Andrew Jackson.

1803
JACKSON AND HUTCHINGS

The Jackson and Hutchings store offered an assortment of goods that met many needs. The most popular items with customers were fabrics, thread, buttons, ribbon, and related materials to make clothing, but they also bought hardware, harnesses, saddles, hand tools, rum, and whiskey. The store sold housewares and a variety of other merchandise including shoe brushes, penknives, wool cards, trunks, fur hats, Bibles, hymnbooks, loaf sugar, playing cards, slates, and chalk.

A Time Line History Celebrating the Bicentennial of Gallatin, Tennessee

Courtesy of U.S. Treasury Department
A view of Albert Gallatin statue.

1813 John H. Bowen elected to Congress. • Volunteers depart for Natchez and below. • Itinerant preacher Lorenzo Dow speaks in Gallatin. • General William Hall and staff officers contest General Andrew Jackson's interpretation of the term of enlistment for their troops.

1815 The *Tennessean* appears as first local newspaper. • The Gallatin, Tennessee Bank receives charter. • General Assembly incorporates town of Gallatin. • Volunteers return after battle of New Orleans.

1817 The General Assembly reorganizes the town government, providing for mayor and seven aldermen. • Gallatin Inn, owned by David Shelby, opens on Public Square. • The *Columbian* is second Gallatin newspaper.

1819 Investors develop first privately owned subdivision, fifty acres. • General James Winchester and his son Marcus take lead in developing the city of Memphis, Tennessee.

1820 Cotillion parties attract dancers to Capt. John Mitchell's ballroom. • Elisha Long produces 300,000 bricks per year at his local brickyard.

1821 Leaving the presidency of Transmontania Academy, John Hall opens Pericles Academy on East Franklin Street extended.

1822 John H. Bowen dies with his house, now known as Trousdale Place, unfinished.

1824 Gallatin Female Academy opens.

1825 Jockey Club organizes and announces races.

1826 Marcus Winchester becomes mayor of Memphis.

1827 Robert Desha is elected to Congress.

Courtesy of Allen Haynes Collection
The Robert M. Boyers Building, built circa 1814.

29

Gallatin 200

1832
Bucket Brigade

"Be it enacted by the mayor & aldermen . . . that each & every person owning a dwelling or store-house (except such houses [as] are usually termed cabbins) shall furnish the same with two fire buckets, that each & every person owning a tavern . . . shall furnish the same with three fire buckets, and that each & every person owning a cabbin, shop or office shall furnish the same with one fire bucket." The buckets were to be made of "leather of the usual form and size" and shall be placed "in that part of his, her or their houses where they can be most easily obtained in case of an alarm or fire."

Minutes of the City Council

1828 Voters elect Andrew Jackson president of the United States. • City paves Main Street. • First Presbyterian Church organizes congregation.

1829 Eliza Allen marries Tennessee Governor Sam Houston, but in a matter of weeks, leaves him never to return for reasons that she does not publicly disclose. • The First Methodist Church is established. • The Sumner County Temperance Society organizes with large Gallatin membership.

1830 Gallatin has a population of 666 persons, 234 of whom are black. Most of the blacks are in slavery with only about ten or twelve free. • Stage service to Carthage is offered twice each week. Nashville-Lexington mail stages pass and repass through Gallatin three times each week.

Blythewood, built circa 1815.

By James W. Thomas

A Time Line History Celebrating the Bicentennial of Gallatin, Tennessee

1831 William Hall gains seat in Congress.

1832 Andrew Jackson wins reelection to presidency. • Isaac Franklin begins construction of residence on his Fairvue plantation. • New local newspaper, the *Guardian*, begins publication. • Aldermen seek money from the county to pave "the rest of the public square." • Publisher discontinues Gallatin *Journal*; reopens to publish new Gallatin *Union*.

1833 Balie Peyton is elected to Congress. • Local whites establish branch of African Colonization Society. • Aldermen vote to remove market house from the Public Square and relocate it to town lot number thirteen near the head of the spring at corner of South Water and Smith Streets. City will extend pavement of East Main Street to the corporate limits, i.e., "the far corner of the stray pen."

1834 Peyton becomes an early promoter of the Whig Party after breaking with President Jackson. • Public meeting at courthouse elects officers for the fire engine company.

Courtesy of Crutcher Studio

Cragfont, completed in 1802.

1835 Voters reelect Balie Peyton to Congress.

1836 The General Assembly charters Gallatin Turnpike Company and grants a charter of incorporation to the Gallatin Female Academy. • Volunteers leave for the Seminole War in Florida.

1835
CLARA BROWN

Born in slavery near Gallatin in 1800, Clara Brown was a member of a family that in 1835 was sold at auction and scattered to the four winds. Manumitted in 1857, Clara began searching for a daughter reported to have gone west. Setting out from Leavenworth, Kansas, in a wagon train, she was one of six women but the only African American. She discovered quickly that the men would pay to have their clothing washed, and she began laundering on the trail. By the time the wagons reached Central City, Colorado, she may have been the wealthiest member of the train. Clara remained there and continued in the laundry business, but her age and the harsh weather conditions forced her to move to Denver in 1880. Central City friends named a chair in the famous Central City Opera House for her. She was a member of the Colorado Society of Pioneers.

GALLATIN 200

Trousdale Place, built circa 1822, front view.

Courtesy of Crutcher Studio

Trousdale Place, rear façade.

By Allen Haynes

A Time Line History Celebrating the Bicentennial of Gallatin, Tennessee

1837 Citizens welcome the Seminole War volunteers' return. • County replaces original courthouse with new one on Public Square. • Eliza Allen and Sam Houston divorce is final. • Isaac Franklin dies and his executor incorporates Isaac Franklin Institute. • City agrees for Gallatin Turnpike Company to tie into westernmost end of Main Street. • Legislature charters three local turnpike companies: Gallatin and Ridge; Gallatin, Hartsville, and Carthage; and Red River.

1838 Local farmers organize the Sumner County Agricultural Society. • Sumner Female Academy succeeds Gallatin Female Academy. • Stage lines operate on regular schedules to and from Nashville, Hartsville, and Carthage. • *The Cumberland Farmer*, the city's first magazine, begins publishing. • Aldermen abolish office of treasurer and assign duties to recorder calling the enlarged office "treasurer and recorder."

1839 City replaces its three public water pumps with new ones.

1840 After the King Solomon Lodge of 1808 surrenders its charter in the late 1830s, a new fraternity is created: King Solomon Lodge No. 94, F.&A.M. • Newspaper advertisements in 1840 show a variety of businesses and

Courtesy of Colorado Historical Society

Clara Brown.

First Presbyterian Church, built in 1836–37.

By Allen Haynes

Gallatin 200

Courtesy of Tennessee Historical Society
Governor William Hall.

Courtesy of Kenneth C. Thomson Jr. Collection.
The Robert M. Boyers House begun circa 1825.

Fairvue built in 1832.

Courtesy of Walter T. Durham Collection.

professions in town. There were merchants, grocers, tailors, cabinetmakers, saddlers, tinners, coppersmiths, blacksmiths, silversmiths, a brick maker, a hatter, a tanner, wagon makers, carpenters, a dentist, medical doctors, confectioners, hotel and inn keepers, a paper mill, and several lawyers.

1841 A literary magazine, *The Southron*, publishes Vol. 1, No. 1. • Aldermen pass ordinance prohibiting the hitching of horses and mules to the courthouse or hitching them within the market house. • Parts of Main and Water Streets are macadamized; property owners along the improved sections are required to install appropriate sidewalks and gutters. • An ordinance is adopted requiring slaves who move freely around town at nights or Sundays to have written pass from their "master or mistress."

By Allen Haynes

Charles Trousdale house of 1837.

1842 The Josephus Conn Guilds complete construction of their plantation house Rose Mont. • Aldermen investigate the cost of digging a public well on the west side of town.

1843 District voters elect Joseph H. Peyton to Congress. • Balie Peyton produces Peyton's Stakes at Nashville and captures attention of international thoroughbred fanciers.

1844 James K. Polk is elected president.

1845 Howard Lodge, No. 13, International Organization of Odd Fellows, receives charter. •

1847
MEXICAN WAR MONUMENT

In the autumn of 1846, a group of Nashvillians launched a promotion to raise a monument to the Tennessee soldiers of the Mexican War, and Gallatin citizens rallied to support the project with a generous subscription of funds. After comparable enthusiasm for the project did not materialize in the capital city, the Gallatin supporters erected a monument in the public cemetery here to honor their own. The names of fifty-four Sumner County soldiers who died in Mexico or who died from war-related causes after returning home are inscribed on its base panels.

GALLATIN 200

1853
WILLIAM TROUSDALE

Awaiting a ship in New York City to take him to an ambassadorial assignment in Brazil in 1853, former governor William Trousdale wrote home to his daughter Louisa of the purposeful life he observed there.

When I contrast the active, bustling life of these Yankees with the dull idle monotonous life of the people of Gallatin it seems to me that a visit here would awaken them from their slumbers and serve them with an energy that is very much wanting. Here each man carries his watch and all his operations are governed by time. Each one's motion is quick and energetic.

J. H. Peyton is reelected to Congress but dies before House convenes.

1846 Congress declares war on Mexico. • Local young men rush to volunteer for military service.

1847 William Trousdale is brevetted Brigadier General at battle of Chapultepec in Mexico. • Legislature charters Long Hollow Turnpike Company.

1848 Appreciative citizens erect Mexican War Monument in Gallatin cemetery. • Colonel Thomas Boyers is a founder and charter member of the Tennessee Historical Society.

1849 Cholera epidemic is devastating. • William Trousdale is elected governor of Tennessee. • Balie Peyton accepts presidential appointment as U.S. minister to Chile. • Young men rush for California gold. • Gallatin and Cairo Turnpike Company receives charter.

1850 Investors organize local cotton factory. • Population of city reaches 1,200.

1851 Louisville & Nashville Railroad will be built through Gallatin. • Henry J. Barker opens new foundry and machine shop to manufacture cast iron plows. • Governor Trousdale loses bid for reelection.

1852 Cholera strikes again.

1853 William Trousdale becomes minister to Brazil. • Gallatin and Coles Ferry Turnpike receives charter.

1854 Spencer's Flour Mills set up. • Jonas Nickelson purchases Barker's foundry.

Foxland Hall of 1836, later remodeled.

Courtesy of Gallatin Chamber of Commerce

36

A Time Line History Celebrating the Bicentennial of Gallatin, Tennessee

Courtesy of Tennessee State Library and Archives
Governor William Trousdale.

By James W. Thomas
Harrison Barracks, built circa 1840, was first a carriage factory.

Courtesy of Crutcher Studio
Levy Ring built this house about 1841.

37

GALLATIN 200

1862
FEAR GRIPPED GALLATIN

On February 18, 1862, as Gallatin awaited the arrival of Union Army troops after the fall of Fort Donelson, eighteen-year-old Laura Williams wrote to her brother in the Confederate Army. She reported excitement and fear on every hand.

The men all looked like their last moments had come. Women and children were flying in every direction. Some left their homes and everything else to fly to some place of safety. . . . Yesterday everybody was huddled around the streets expecting them to come. . . . I just wish you could . . . see how scared the people are. . . . Men are worse scared than women. Some of the men (be it said to their shame) did raise several white flags in town.

—Letter courtesy of Kenneth Calvin Thomson Jr.

1855 Middle Tennessee State Fair entertains thousands here.

1856 The Sumner Female Academy becomes Howard Female Institute, later Howard College. • Thomas Boyers founds and edits Gallatin *Examiner*.

1858 The Louisville and Nashville Railroad is completed with depot here. • First Baptist Church organizes and meets in the Odd Fellows Hall.

1860 Abraham Lincoln is elected president. • Secession sentiment grows. • Trying to head off war, Balie Peyton works to organize and promote Constitutional Union Party. • A Howard Female Institute student news and literary publication, *The Bud of Thought*, appears with strongly pro-Union sentiment. • First gas lighting is turned on. • First Baptist Church on East Main Street is built and dedicated.

1861 Civil War begins. • Tennessee declares independence from the Union and affiliates with the Confederacy. • Volunteer companies enlist. • Howard Female Institute closes. •

1862
BATTLE OF GALLATIN

The battle of Gallatin was fought between Gen. R. W. Johnson's Federal cavalry and Col. John Hunt Morgan's Confederate horsemen on the morning of August 21, 1862. Approaching from Castalian Springs, the Federal force of about eight hundred men met seven hundred Confederates at the junction of the Hartsville and Scottsville Pikes. For the first two hours, General Johnson's men seemed to prevail, but Colonel Morgan's cavalry rallied and drove them back toward Castalian Springs. Unable to contain Morgan, Johnson turned his troops toward Cairo where they made a final stand while perhaps 450 of their number escaped across the river. The Union general and his remaining men then surrendered. Morgan reported Federal losses as sixty-four killed, one hundred wounded, and two hundred prisoners. His own losses were five killed, eighteen wounded, and two missing. After the battle that lasted from daylight until noon, Morgan's victorious cavalry withdrew to Hartsville.

A Time Line History Celebrating the Bicentennial of Gallatin, Tennessee

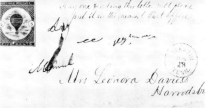

Buffalo Balloon drops airmail. By James W. Thomas

Partners organize Sumner Armory to make rifles in shop on north side of Red River Road at the railroad. • Confederates set up Camp Trousdale near Portland, giving it the name of Governor Trousdale. • In an example of split sentiments in same family, Balie Peyton remains loyal to Union; son Balie joins Confederate Army.

1862 Union Army arrives in town unopposed; city and county government cease operating. • Colonel Morgan's Confederate Cavalry takes, leaves, and retakes Gallatin for short periods. • Morgan wins battle of Gallatin in five-hour cavalry clash. • Union Army establishes garrison. • Military Governor Johnson banishes Josephus Conn Guild to Union prison at Fort Mackinac, Michigan.

1863 Union sends Gen. Eleazor Paine to command railroad guard and build Fort Thomas. He quickly becomes focus of citizens' wrath. • Rebel guerrillas rip up tracks, harass the guards. • Union Army threatens to burn town if residents continue to aid guerrillas. • First former slaves enlist in Union Army here in the 14th U.S. Colored Infantry Regiment. • Union garrison publishes newspaper. • Citizens and army care for four thousand sick and wounded Federal soldiers from battles below Nashville.

1864 Abraham Lincoln secures reelection to presidency with Andrew Johnson vice president. • General Paine is transferred. • Army foragers active. • Union fortifications are put in place

Mexican War Monument. By Allen Haynes

39

GALLATIN 200

1868

JOSEPH SMITH FOWLER

An outstanding president of Howard Female Institute was the pro-Union Joseph Smith Fowler until the pro-Southern board of trust, fearing for his family's safety, advised him to "go North" on the eve of the Civil War. When Andrew Johnson became military governor in 1862, Fowler was called to Nashville where he was state comptroller until the end of the war when he was elected to represent Tennessee in the United States Senate. During his term as comptroller, he exercised protective care of the holdings of the state library, preserving them largely intact. While in the Senate, he voted to acquit President Andrew Johnson of the impeachment charges brought by the House.

to guard South Tunnel. • Only sworn loyalists are eligible to vote in Tennessee. • Cannon firing from battle of Nashville is heard.

1865 Confederate Army General Lee surrenders at Appomattox. • President Lincoln assassinated; Andrew Johnson becomes president. • Artillerymen fire twenty-one-gun farewell salute to Lincoln at Fort Thomas. • Army relaxes control of city and county government. • Ellis Harper's guerrillas surrender. • Surviving Confederate soldiers return home. • Lawlessness concerns blacks and whites. • 101st U.S. Colored Infantry garrisons Fort Thomas. • Freedmen's Bureau opens local office. • Freedmen's schools enroll 581 pupils. • Mayor and aldermen meet for first time since January 4, 1862. • Joseph Smith Fowler, Unionist and former president of Howard Female Institute, is elected to represent Tennessee in the United States Senate. • Constitutional amendment frees slaves. • Smallpox rages.

1866 Black Baptist and Methodist congregations organize. • Former slaves establish Sumner County Colored Agricultural Fair Association. • Radical Unionists, white and black, control city government. • Howard Female Institute reopens. • Henry Fitzgerald begins operation of cotton mill at the end of Factory Lane. • City school commissioners turn the common school building over to the trustees of Transmontania Academy.

1867 In special election, blacks achieve first representation on city Board of Aldermen. Outgoing aldermen protest. • Gallatin and Lebanon Railroad Company is proposed. • Aldermen object to carpetbagger representative trying to pass act increasing land area of town fourfold.

1868 Voters elect Ulysses S. Grant president of the United States. • Local Radicals and former secessionists begin to make peace. • Hilary W. Key leads former slaves in building a Methodist Episcopal church on Blythe Street. • Other former slaves locate Baptist Church on Winchester Street. • Eagle Woolen Mills begins operations on Railroad Avenue.

1869 Voters sweep Radicals, black and white, out of local offices. • "Peace of the town is greatly improved." • Fire ravages thirteen buildings on west side Public Square.

1870 Population of Gallatin is 2,123. • City will install gas street lights.

1871 City sells market house; will erect "horse racks" on old jail lot. • Survey and plat of city is made; all streets and alleys receive names.

1872 Fitzgerald's cotton mill goes up in flames; will be rebuilt. • All businesses close for William Trousdale's funeral.

1873 Big cholera outbreak results in 120 deaths; there were "very few cases" among those who observed "proper hygienic precautions." City will pay for medicine

A Time Line History Celebrating the Bicentennial of Gallatin, Tennessee

prescribed for charity cases. • Mayor proclaims citywide cleanup. • Aldermen authorize city recorder to spend eight dollars for new minute book. • City wants all houses with a smallpox patient inside to put up a yellow flag outside. • If a viable free school can be established, city will give certain lots it owns for building site. • New horse-drawn fire engine called the Champion Fire Extinguisher is purchased by city for two thousand dollars.

1874 Local attorney and former State Attorney General Charles R. Head is elected to Congress but dies eight days later. • Coed Neophogen College succeeds Howard Female Institute. • Southern Methodists build new house of worship on West Main Street.

1875 The Southern Blacking Manufacturing Company is in production. • J. W. Walton Flouring Mills operate on Blythe Street.

By James W. Thomas

Oakland, built about 1848.

Gallatin 200

1877
First Airmail

Ascending at Nashville, the hot air balloon *Buffalo* made the first recorded delivery of airmail in the Southeast when it dropped packets of letters at Gallatin on June 18, 1877. Aeronaut Samuel A. King then landed the balloon and local citizens toasted him and his six passengers in a victory celebration at Hotel Sumner on West Main Street. On June 18, 1977, the United States Postal Service issued a commemorative stamp and first day cover marking the centennial anniversary of the event.

1876 Four or five local families attend the Philadelphia Exposition celebrating the one hundredth birthday of America's independence.

1877 The *Buffalo*, a hot air balloon, brings first airmail to Gallatin.

1878 Neophogen College yields to new board and president who reinstate Howard Female Institute. • A detailed map of Sumner County is published by D. C. Beers and Company, Philadelphia, Pennsylvania.

1879 Howard Female College is chosen as name for the former Howard Female Institute and will remain so for the life of the school.

1880 Population of town is 1,938. • Gas works sets up on Franklin Street to furnish gas for public and private lighting.

1882 New Yorker Charles Reed purchases Fairvue for use as thoroughbred horse breeding farm. • Voters elect William B. Bate, former Confederate general and Gallatin newspaper editor, governor of Tennessee. • City will pay for smallpox vaccinations for everyone within city limits. • Mayor and Sanitary Committee request that everyone ill with smallpox be taken to the "Old Race Track Grounds" where they will be treated by two medical doctors chosen by the city and cared for in improvised quarters in the stables.

1883 City awards contract to build a workhouse. • Biennial election of mayor and aldermen replaces annual balloting. • A school district is organized for Gallatin.

1884 Bate is reelected governor. • Chesapeake and Nashville Railroad Company is incorporated; will branch northeastward off L&N at Gallatin. • City establishes board of education to operate public schools for white and black scholastic population made up of 129 white males, 167 white females, 149 black males, and 160 black females.

Oakley, built in 1852.

By Allen Haynes

1885 Cumberland Telephone and Telegraph Company contracts to furnish telephone service to city. At first they will furnish and service a total of seven telephones at locations to be selected by the mayor and fire chief.

1886 Contractors finish the Chesapeake and Nashville Railroad line from Gallatin to the Kentucky state line. • Fire destroys Tomkins buildings on south side Public Square; a falling brick wall results in death of one of the owners. • City appropriates ten thousand dollars for land and building costs for public schools.

1887 The Middle and East Tennessee Central Railroad is under construction from its intersection with the C&N Railroad at Bledsoe Creek to Hartsville. • William B. Bate is elected to the United States Senate. • City charter is amended to provide authority to erect a suitable waterworks and to finance same by issuing bonds.

1889 Public school enrollment is 204 "white" at Main Street School and 184 "colored" at South Street School.

1890 Population is 2,078. • Ordinance is passed making it a misdemeanor to ride a bicycle, velocipede, or tricycle on city sidewalks.

1891 The Pythian College receives charter from General Assembly; purchases

The church of 1860, First Baptist, East Main.

Courtesy of Walter T. Durham Collection

1890
PROTECTING HORSES

A city ordinance of 1890 made it a misdemeanor to fly kites, throw missiles, play ball, or do any act, or make a noise in any public street or elsewhere likely to frighten horses or alarm or injure any person, or impede the free passage of vehicles and footmen along the streets.

Another made it a misdemeanor for any person to drive, with the intention and for the purpose of breaking any young horse or mare colt, or horse or mare of any age, or for the purpose of training or speeding the said animal upon the Public Square, or upon Water Street, or Main Street, or Railroad Avenue.

Gallatin 200

Courtesy of Tennessee Historical Society
Joseph Smith Fowler.

twenty-five-acre campus site on west side of Dobbins Pike, one mile north of the Public Square. • Charles Reed pays $100,000 for the thoroughbred St. Blaise, highest price heretofore paid for an American horse.

1892 Ordinance is passed ruling that horses and other animals are not to be left unhitched on the Public Square. • Lewd women are prohibited by ordinance from "walking or loitering" about the streets after 8:00 P.M.

1893 Workhouse prisoners are given the task of beating thirty bushels of rock per day and will be allowed 11½ cents per bushel to credit their fines. • Ordinance is adopted to erect waterworks.

1894 City offers reward of one hundred dollars for information leading to the arrest of the person who inflicted the injuries that caused the death of city marshal F. H. Lassiter. • Knights of Pythias lay cornerstone for main building of Pythian College.

1895 City purchases water tank and windmill to sprinkle the streets of the Public Square and Main Street.

1896 Promoters abandon plans for Pythian College.

Union soldiers on Public Square, 19th O.V.I., 1862.

Courtesy of Ohio Historical Society

44

A Time Line History Celebrating the Bicentennial of Gallatin, Tennessee

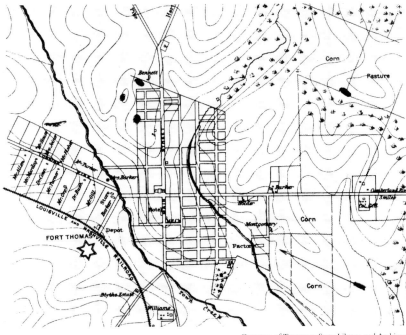

Courtesy of Tennessee State Library and Archives

Fort Thomas location map, 1865.

Courtesy of Mrs. Mary Stewart Collection

Hilary W. Key.

1897 Lightning strikes First Baptist Church, East Main, and ensuing fire burns it to the ground. • Voters choose Edward Ward Carmack for seat in Congress. He was born in Castalian Springs and later maintained close ties to Gallatin. • City will build water system using a pump station at the Cumberland River to supply homes and businesses.

1898 The United States declares war on Spain over the question of Cuban independence. • Baptists rebuild church on East Main street site.

1899 Perkins Drug Store opens on Public Square. • Phosphate mining is conducted north of town at foot of the ridge. • Devastating fire sweeps entire south side of Public Square. • "Electric Light Bonds" are authorized to finance erection of an "electric light plant" by the city. • Gallatin Spoke Works makes wooden spokes for vehicle wheels.

1900. First water mains laid. Population is 2,409. • City grants right to Cumberland Telephone and Telegraph Company to erect, operate, and maintain overhead structures along streets and alleys to facilitate the transmission of communications by wire.

1901 Edward Ward Carmack wins seat in U.S. Senate.

1903 Electric Power Plant begins full operations; will produce enough electricity for 1,500 light bulbs burning simultaneously. • Bowen's Lodge No. 21, Knights of Pythias celebrates its twenty-fifth anniversary February 27, 1903, at Castle Hall. • W. W. Fidler's Mastodon Fusee Minstrels in town to raise funds to equip a local baseball team. • Gallatin votes out saloons. •Aldermen pass ordinance prohibiting the operation of a "blind tiger or other place or device for the unlawful sale of whiskey, ale, beer, or any intoxicating liquors."

1904 Hawkins School opens as a private preparatory school, C. E. Hawkins headmaster.

1905 W. G. Schamberger will erect handsome three-story block to include lodge rooms, opera house, and business houses at southeast corner of Public Square and East Main Street. • Gallatin Athletic Club organizes. • Nashville investors plan to build

Gallatin 200

1905
Speed Limit 10 mph

On July 6, 1905, the City Council passed an ordinance stipulating that no person, driver, or operator in charge of any automobile, motor car, bicycle, motorcycle, or any other vehicle propelled by steam, gasoline, or electricity, operated on any public street in the town of Gallatin, shall drive, operate, move, or permit the same to be driven, operated, or moved at a rate of speed to exceed *10 miles per hour* within the corporate limits of the town of Gallatin.

Interurban Railway. • United States Senator William Brimage Bate dies in Washington. • Gallatin shops of C&N build passenger coach. • Local firm established to manufacture pins used for insulator globes on electric light, telephone, and telegraph poles. • Three separate newspapers now publish from locations on east side of Public Square.

1906 Gallatin merchants begin offering annual millinery displays. • Lots sell at auction in new Eastland subdivision. • Moving picture exhibition on the Square draws large crowd. • Chesapeake and Nashville Railroad connecting Scottsville to Gallatin with branch to Hartsville is acquired by L&N. • Deposits of the three Gallatin banks exceed $488,000 in total.

1907 Board of Trade is organized with sixty members.

Fitzgerald House, 1866–69.

By Allen Haynes

A Time Line History Celebrating the Bicentennial of Gallatin, Tennessee

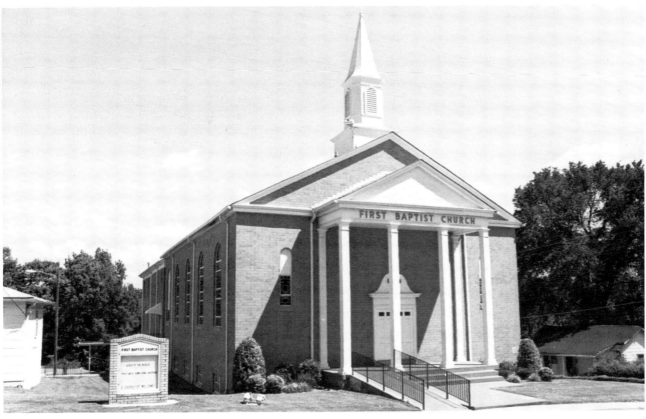

By Allen Haynes

First Baptist Church, Winchester Street.

1908 Local women establish the Civic Improvement League and sponsor community wide cleanup days. • Charles Read sells his two thousand-acre Fairvue farm for $75,000. • Support rallies for proposed *Great Highway from the Lakes to the Gulf* through Gallatin. • Movie patrons see "The Holy City" at the Electric Theatre. The film is 1,800 feet in length; admission ten cents. • Sumner County Fair opens its fifth annual exhibition on West Main Street. • Flames consume W. L. Baker's Carriage Shop on North Water. • Fletcher Hotel foundation nearly complete just off the Public Square on the south side of East Main Street.

1909 Vaudeville plays at Schamberger's new auditorium. • Local editor says "muddy condition of the Public Square is a disgrace," and calls for new courthouse to replace the 1837 structure. • Gentlemen's Shakespeare Club meets. • Sumner Training School stockholders meet. • Court decrees sale of Sumner Phosphate Company, marking the demise of local phosphate mining. • Civil Improvement League to discuss sprinkling streets during summer months to control dust. • Commencement exercises at Main Street High School mark twenty-two years of public school system in Gallatin. • Opportunity for Gallatin to be the site for Middle Tennessee Normal, more recently Middle Tennessee State University, is lost when bond issue for one hundred thousand dollar seed money is rejected in county-wide referendum. • New owners take over at Gallatin (flour) Mills on Red River Road. • City Council hears proposition to build railroad from Gallatin to the Cumberland River, about three miles. • Automobile line (bus service) opens between Gallatin and Dixon

47

Courtesy of Gallatin Chamber of Commerce

Key Stewart Methodist Episcopal Church.

Springs. • Lightning strikes Jones Hotel located at corner of Railroad Avenue and North Water Street. Sixteen guests in the building at the time were shocked but none seriously injured. • S. J. Fletcher of Indianapolis, Indiana, and builder of new Fletcher Hotel, dies while visiting Gallatin on Christmas Day.

1910 Plans ready for proposed loose leaf tobacco sales warehouse. City agrees to furnish light and water for ten years without charge. • Fletcher Hotel will not be completed by heirs but is sold to a Springfield, Tennessee, banker for $13,700. • Main Street High School to build additional space for 150 students. • W. N. Robertson & Company, furniture dealers, entertain ladies with a "Jap o chi no" tea. Young lady servers wear Japanese costumes. Gallatin Dry Goods Company treats customers to music by an Italian band from Nashville. • Fire destroys contents of H. W. Person's

---

1910

JEFFRIES-JOHNSON PRIZEFIGHT

On July 10, 1910, Mayor W. G. Schamberger asked the City Council to pass an ordinance that would prohibit the local exhibition of moving pictures of the Jeffries-Johnson prizefight. Six days before at Reno, Nevada, Jack Johnson, a black fighter, had won the world heavyweight championship in a fifteen-round match with James J. Jeffries, a white boxer and former champion then trying to make a comeback.

A Time Line History Celebrating the Bicentennial of Gallatin, Tennessee

1910
A PULL ALL TOGETHER

On January 18, 1910, the City Council voted to furnish free electric lights and water as an enticement for the location of a burley tobacco sales floor here. In response to this important vote, Mayor W. G. Schamberger spoke of the need for cooperation:

Building upon all the good things we now have, catching the spirit of progress for which the age is rife, let us trust that every department of our little government may work in perfect harmony, and let us make a long pull, a strong pull, and a pull all together for a better and *Greater Gallatin*.

bookstore on Public Square. • Mrs. Prudence Dresser's two music schools, here and in Nashville, earn acclaim from critic for New York *Musical Observer*. • "A new and greater Howard College," new president Walter Aurelius Ingram promises. • Professor Offitt's Cornet Band furnishes music for Sumner Colored Fair. • The Gallatin-Nashville Interurban announces all stock necessary for its construction has been sold; surveying party is in the field. City will grant rights-of-way over certain streets to be used by Interurban. • City population is 2,399.

1911 Auto Club organizes. • A highway from Nashville to Louisville, Kentucky, through Gallatin, Scottsville, Glasgow, Bardstown, and Lincoln farm is fast becoming a reality. • Forepaugh-Sells Brothers Circus is largest ever in town; attracts attendance of between five thousand and seven thousand persons. Parade was a mile in length. • Over one hundred medical doctors attend Middle Tennessee Medical Association meeting here. • Citizens rally to support the financially distressed Hawkins School.

1912 Local group receives charter for electric railway line from Gallatin to points in Kentucky, but undertaking dies at that point. • Veterans of battle of Shiloh gather at Courthouse to commemorate fiftieth anniversary of the battle. • County purchases Nashville-Gallatin Turnpike for twenty-five thousand dollars; toll gates removed all the way east to Bransford. • City builds new electric power plant to accommodate expanding demands.

1913 Mass meeting discusses establishment of public hay market and hitching lot for the town. • Interurban up and running; four cars carry twenty-five hundred passengers on first Sunday. • Businessmen organize the Commercial Club. • Deadlocked three to three for 108 ballots, the six-man City Board of

First United Methodist Church.

By Allen Haynes

49

Education elected Captain C. S. Douglass superintendent of schools on the 109th ballot by a vote of 4 to 2. • Public Square improvements include electric street lights to be mounted on courthouse and a "sanitary drinking fountain for livestock" on east side. • Gallatin merchants will pay ferry tolls for Wilson Countians coming across the river to shop or trade. • City and county purchase Fletcher Hotel building for joint use as a high school.

1914 Gallatin Church of Christ erects new house of worship on corner of East Main and Boyers Street. • High School is named Allen-Trousdale High School; yellow and green adopted as school colors.

1915 Name changed from Allen-Trousdale to Central High School.

1916 The Cumberland Telephone Company will erect a new telephone exchange building adjoining the Interurban Railway station on West Main Street. • Chautauqua ends; is called "great success." • Franklin, Kentucky Boosters celebrate July 4 in Gallatin with parade, speeches, and other activities.

1917 U.S. Congress declares war on Germany. •

Hotel Sumner.

Courtesy of Allen Haynes Collection

1918
Sleepwalking to Music

Francis Craig, popular music composer whose dance orchestra frequently originated NBC radio broadcasts through WSM, Nashville, during the 1930s and 1940s, was a young child when his father, R. J. Craig, was pastor at First Methodist Church in 1913–1914. At the height of his career, Francis enjoyed relating an experience that he had while living with his parents in the parsonage on East Main Street immediately east of Howard College campus.

He recalled that he wanted to attend a public concert scheduled for the college on an early summer evening, but his parents would not allow it and sent him upstairs to bed. Listening to the faint strains of music through his open bedroom window, he finally drifted off to sleep. A few moments later, attracted by the music, he arose from bed, walked in his sleep toward the music, and fell through the open window to the ground below landing on his head.

With the wink of an eye, he would conclude, "I have been a musician ever since."

A Time Line History Celebrating the Bicentennial of Gallatin, Tennessee

Community rallies in big send-off for soldiers headed to war in Europe. • The Nashville-Gallatin Interurban round trip ticket sells for one dollar. • Fire destroys C. E. Northrup & Sons planing mill on North Water Street. • Construction is set for new post office on East Main. • Locals call for gray brick instead of red for new post office; want tile floor instead of proposed concrete. • Williams School succeeds Hawkins School with Sam Williams as principal.

1918 A patriotic gathering at the courthouse hears "reasons and causes" of the war. Spirit of patriotism is evident on every side. • Sumner County is limited to wood fuel for duration of war. • Cumberland River flood is biggest since 1882. High water blocks highway and Interurban travel to Nashville. • New post office opens. • Allies, Central Powers declare Armistice on November 11 and war ends.

1920 Treaty of Versailles marks formal close of World War I. • Milk producers build and open a creamery as cooperative venture located on Railroad Avenue. • Suddarth Phonograph Company "opens doors" to local music lovers at Public Square store. • Williams Training School, successor to Hawkins School, graduates first senior class. • City installs chlorine gas plant to purify the water supply "of all disease germs," but there is still need for a filter system "to clear water of mud and other impurities when the river is up." • Mrs. W. Y. Allen and Mrs. Prudence S. Dresser accept appointment to state women's suffrage committee. • Gallatin population is 2,757 up from 2,399 in 1910.

Courtesy of Sumner County Archives

Horse-drawn fire truck and crew, circa 1895.

GALLATIN 200

Howard Female Institute. By E. M. Stark

Sumner County census shows 27,708. • Sumner Auto Club encourages driver courtesy; seeks to improve traffic congestion around courthouse. • Author and lecturer Opie Read visits former Gallatin home. • City contracts with Tennessee Power Company for electricity to be supplied over line built from Nashville to a new substation here. Gallatin Power Plant to be kept for use in emergency situations. • Central High School wins accreditation by Southern Association of Colleges and Secondary Schools.

1921 Ford and Duke Tobacco Warehouse nears completion on Gray Street; is largest building in town, three stories high with eighty-three thousand square feet of floor space. • Hub Perdue becomes manager of Nashville Vols professional baseball team. • Fire destroys Farmers Loose Leaf Tobacco Warehouse and its contents of about two hundred thousand pounds of tobacco. It was one of three such warehouses in town. • Public mass meeting protests proposed increase in telephone rates. • Guests ride to the hounds in fox chase on John M. Branham's estate Foxland Hall. • Fire hits restaurant, buggy company, and pressing club on north side of Public Square. • Current flows in from Tennessee Power Company. • Patrons conduct fund drive to complete third floor of Central High School. • State will erect historical marker on Hartsville Pike at site of Isaac Bledsoe's Fort. • Fire destroys the buildings that house shoe shop, the county garage, a tin shop, and the *Examiner-Tennessean* printing office. • Local businessmen join hands to recruit industry.

1922 Surveys begin for reconstruction of the Jackson Highway from Gallatin to Nashville. • Appearing in chieftain's costume and "full war paint," Sioux Chief Red Fox entertains at Central High School. • Fire engulfs auto repair shop; all equipment and seven automobiles destroyed. • Gallatin Private Institute succeeds Williams Training School in old Hawkins

---

1922
GALLATIN PRIVATE INSTITUTE

By far the greatest heritage of G.P.I. boys is the G.P.I. spirit. This spirit is a personal devotion to the ideals of the school; and the great ideal is character. No character is possible without the simultaneous development of body, mind and soul. . . . This spirit has its source in the three-fold purposes of the school—namely, Strong Discipline, Hard Work, Fair Play.

—*G.P.I. Yearbook 1923*

The core of this building is the former Cumberland Presbyterian Church built in 1889, East Main Street.

By Allen Haynes

facilities and opens with H. K. Bowen, principal. • Charles R. Tomkins moves radio receiver from his home to his office on the Public Square where it can be heard by "all who care to attend." • Howard College closes after exhausting its financial resources. • Cornerstone is set for new Union High School on East Winchester Street for African Americans in Sumner County. • For first time Santa Claus arrives by airplane for Christmas festival. • Sumner Medical Society petitions County Court to create a county health department.

1923 Gallatin Rotary Club is born. • Colored Knights of Pythias will erect lodge hall on site of recently-burned livery stable on North Water Street. • Storm strips roofs from Chero-Cola Bottling Plant and David Kregarman Department Store and damages several other buildings; interrupts electric and telephone services. • Mrs. Mannie Lanier of Gallatin will seek election as county trustee; is first woman to announce for public office in Sumner County. • Handsome stone structure will house First and Peoples Bank on corner of the Square and North Water. • A Nashville bank purchases site on south side Public Square for branch

GALLATIN 200

1925
FORMER SLAVE DIES AT 110

On June 5, 1924, the *Sumner County News* reported the death of a former slave of the Peach Valley community, now a part of Gallatin. Bettie Baker died at the age of 110. Ninety-eight years before, Isaac Franklin of Fairvue plantation purchased her, her brothers and sisters, and her parents from John Washington, adopted son of President George Washington, in Virginia. Brought to Gallatin, they lived at Fairvue until sometime after Franklin's death. After emancipation in 1865, Bettie Baker settled in Peach Valley.

office. • Typhoid fever strikes community. Health Department says typhoid cannot be stopped until citizens are willing to spend thirty thousand dollars for a modern filtration plant that could furnish five hundred thousand gallons of sparkling clean water every day. Until then, drinking water should be boiled. • Mass meeting of citizens approves expenditures for filtration plant and for "reconstructing" 150,000 square yards of city streets: North and South Water, East and West Main, Public Square, and Railroad Avenue. A later referendum approves both. • County court votes to sell $150,000 in bonds for completion of Jackson Highway from Gallatin to Kentucky state line. • Gillespie Oil Corporation will build refinery near old Fry Tanyard on West Main Street just west of Town Creek. • Fire severely damages grocery store and restaurant near L&N Depot.

1924 Local investors establish a company to manufacture plow handles and will produce three thousand per day. • Exchange Club is formed in Gallatin. • Commercial Club wants electric "white way" to illuminate Public Square. • Desire for industrial employment reflected in unfounded rumors of impending new factories to make brooms, chairs, overalls, and work shirts. • Fire guts Keystone Hotel at corner of North Water and Railroad Avenue. All of twenty-four guests escape safely. • "Aunt" Bettie Baker, 110 years of age and a former slave, dies at her Peach Valley home. • City begins "to asphalt and gutter" Main Streets; some trees will be cut and utility poles moved back. • Gallatin Boosters with Chamber of Commerce band tour neighboring towns. • Sumner Canning Company is in operation; puts out ten thousand cans daily. • Old telephone building that adjoins Central High School is remodeled; the original structure was built of walnut logs which are still in excellent condition. • A filtration plant is built at pumping station. • Chamber of Commerce raises one thousand dollars for Gallatin Private Institute.

Central High School of 1890.

By Allen Haynes

54

A Time Line History Celebrating the Bicentennial of Gallatin, Tennessee

1925 Clothes line factory will open. • Cyclone is fatal to several in northern Sumner County. Emergency hospital is set up here in house on Railroad Avenue. • County paints courthouse yellow with white trim and "pencillings of black." • Editor says city needs lower electric power rates to attract industry. • Dr. Humphrey Bate and his string quartet known as the Possum Hunters play for radio station WDAD at Nashville and soon will be heard over WSM on the Grand Ole Opry. • Train wreck in South Tunnel ignites timbers that support the tunnel; Gallatin Fire Department fought the difficult blaze. • Chamber of Commerce is successful in getting L&N to continue passenger service to Scottsville and Hartsville. • The Gallatin dance orchestra, the Blue Grass Serenaders, broadcasts frequently from radio station WSM, Nashville.

1926 New bus line to Nashville has departures every two hours 8:00 A.M. to 5:00 P.M. • Local golf club organizes. • "White way" lighting around Public Square is in full illumination. • Woodmen of the World bring fifteen hundred people to Gallatin all-day picnic. • Citizens will observe 150th anniversary of the birth of our nation. • Editorial advocates construction of Cumberland River Bridge at either Cole's or Woods Ferry. • Properties of Gallatin Private Institute and Howard

Courtesy of Herb Peck Collection

General William B. Bate.

Artist's rendering of Pythian University.

Courtesy of Walter T. Durham Collection

55

Gallatin 200

1928
Chief Bert Wallace

As late as the 1920s, Gallatin's police force lived in the person of Capt. Bert Wallace whose skill with his billy (stick) became legendary. Although when on duty he wore a holster with a loaded revolver, the stick was his enforcer. Whenever anyone resisted arrest or behaved in any unacceptable way, Captain Bert would say quietly, "Straighten up now. If you don't, I'll have to tap ye." When it came, the tap was authoritative enough to render the recipient very cooperative or very unconscious. Captain Wallace truly spoke softly and carried a big stick.

School will be sold. "Days of small private schools is past unless they have endowment." • Palace Theater and the Roth Jewelry Store have new marquee with seventy-five electric lights. • Dark-Fired Tobacco Association Warehouse, built in 1920 by Ford and Duke of Carthage, completely destroyed by fire that claims two stores across the street and Anderson's Tobacco Warehouse in its rear. • Heavy wind topples historic pecan tree thirty-six inches in diameter on Mrs. Elizabeth Wallace's place north of town on Dobbins Pike. • Flooding the Cumberland River is more than a mile wide at Woods Ferry. Backwater is over the Nashville Pike at Number One and Mansker's Creek; Interurban track inundated at both places.

Sumner Cotton Manufacturing Company.

By James W. Thomas

A Time Line History Celebrating the Bicentennial of Gallatin, Tennessee

1927 Howard College campus and buildings sold to local purchasers who may convert property into apartments. • City purchases Guy Fitzgerald property on West Main for site of combination City Hall and fire station. • City Council agrees to purchase Howard College property with county as half partner. • D. K. Duncan signs contract to build new City Hall and Fire Hall for $13,393. • Owner B. J. Franklin sells Fairvue plantation of 318 acres to Charles B. Rogan of Gallatin for $51,390 at sale attended by four to five thousand people. • J. A. Sloan Company of Columbia, Tennessee, will begin construction of three-story steel and concrete building at L&N Depot to house wholesale grocery operation. Charles C. Parks is manager of Gallatin warehouse. • Franklin Milling Company of Franklin, Kentucky, purchases Gallatin Milling Company property at auction for $18,703. • A private utility, the Kentucky-Tennessee Light and Power Company, purchases Gallatin electrical system and contracts to furnish local electrical needs. • Fire destroys Keen Broom Factory on Lyon Street.

Courtesy of Sumner County Archives

The Jo Horton Fall, *a Cumberland River steamboat owned by Captain Tom Ryman.*

1928 County buys Hawkins School, ten acres and two buildings for $8,020. May build high school there. • Kraft Cheese Company agrees to locate a plant here. A company vice president met with local Chamber of Commerce representatives and final deal was completed in Chicago on February 15. Local plant will receive first milk July 16. • Draughon Business College of Nashville expects to open a branch in former Howard School buildings. • Racehorse breeding may

---

1930
STEEPLECHASE COURSES

George Horine, civil engineer and race track builder left Lexington Kentucky on January 27 for Gallatin with drawings and blueprints for the three courses to be laid out on the property of Grasslands Hunting and Racing Foundation. It is intended to have racing there this year in the autumn. One of the most pretentious undertakings of sportsmen in this country, it combines racing, fox hunting, golf, aviation, swimming, rowing, tennis, polo, etc., with the arrangements of homes and clubs for the members. A membership fee is $10,000 and many subscriptions have already been taken. Work on the tracks is to begin immediately.

—*Sumner County News*,
January 30, 1930.

57

GALLATIN 200

1930
THE GRASSLANDS
INTERNATIONAL STEEPLECHASE

A reporter for *Vogue* magazine was on hand for the inaugural race.

Cars began to stream into the gate at Fairvue at daybreak. Then the outskirts of the course began to teem with human ants—thousands of them. The bookies began to yell, the cameras began to click, jockeys tried to laugh, and owners became grim as the starting moment approached. Banners everywhere bore the brilliant red and yellow colors that marked Grasslands. Out in front lay a great sweep of country. It was all too good to be true—a picture unprecedented in America.

be making a comeback. Famous breeder J. B. McGinn leases farm on Red River Road and brings thoroughbred mares in to begin nursery. • Civic clubs call for public to support establishing a hospital in town. • Floods again hit area. Cumberland River rises twenty feet in less than twenty-four hours.

1929 Legislature passes bill to build river bridge at Woods Ferry with specification that contract must be let within two years. • Sixteen-inch snow clogs traffic; deepest snowfall since 1886. • Local creamery begins manufacture of ice cream. • City places order for American La France fire engine at cost of thirteen thousand dollars. • Three-story addition to Baptist Church on East Main will house Sunday School department at cost of $65,000. • First Methodist Church on West Main celebrates centennial anniversary. • The Sumner County Health Department begins operations on July 1 replacing the Public

Price and Day Stagecoach.

Courtesy of Allen Haynes Collection

A Time Line History Celebrating the Bicentennial of Gallatin, Tennessee

Health Nursing Service. • Public interest in home radio reception is high. • Acting for a group of sportsmen organized as the Southern Grasslands Hunt and Racing Foundation, the Sumner Land Company acquires 1,473 acres in and around the Fairvue plantation between the Nashville Pike and the river. • A few days later stock market crashes.

1930 Grasslands seen as utopia for sportsmen. Foundation plans to convert Fairvue mansion into Bachelor's Hall and construct an inn on Pilot Knob Hill. • Racecourse for steeplechase will be reminiscent of "Old England" as it duplicates the course and jumps at Aintree. • Grasslands wants big highway sign boards along its property lines moved. • State sets aside $250,000 to build highway from Woods Ferry north to Mitchellville. • Communicants dedicate St. John Vianney Catholic Church on North Water. • Sumner County Colored Fair Association moves to new fairgrounds on Blythe Street. • Colonel Robert McCormick, publisher of the *Chicago Tribune*, and a party of guests arrive at Grasslands by seaplane and land on river. • English horses arrive for International Steeplechase; have crossed Atlantic on SS *Minnetonka*. King of Spain will present trophy. • Woods Ferry Bridge contract awarded to a Birmingham firm for $201,859.74. State deposits construction funds in Rogers Caldwell's Bank of Tennessee that defaults within a few days, before withdrawals are made. • A New York horse named Alligator won the Grasslands International Steeplechase. • Mass meeting demands investigation of loss of state funds for Woods Ferry Bridge deposited in Caldwell's Bank of Tennessee; endorses State Senator J. T. Durham, the bridge's sponsor, for speaker of the Senate. • Population reaches 3,050.

1931 R. C. Owen Tobacco Company will move its manufacturing plant from Hartsville to Gallatin. It will occupy the Gallatin

Public Square looking eastward, circa 1909.

By E. M. Stark

1933
CLEAN UP!

Never have I seen our town so cluttered with litter. We have only a small city dump. Drink city water. There is no safe well in Gallatin. Get rid of hogs or other stock within corporation. Have your children vaccinated against typhoid and diphtheria. Gallatin now has 3,643 people. We are growing up so let's get away from this sloppy small town stuff and get our 913 homes cleaned up and ready for hot weather.

—Dr. W. N. Lackey,
City Health Officer

GALLATIN 200

Confederate monument, Trousdale Place.

By Allen Haynes

Milling Company property after the facilities there have been remodeled and enlarged. Expect operations to begin about September 1. • Two new loose-leaf tobacco sales floors are proposed for Gallatin. • Federal government will erect revolving beacon at site of Gallatin Airport on the Frank Sullivan farm west of town on Red River Road. • Plans are underway for a new high school building for Gallatin on old Hawkins School lot. • Workmen begin demolition of old Howard College buildings to clear site for new public Howard Elementary School. • Fire completely destroys two stores on South Water Street. • Kraft-Phenix Cheese Company prepares to manufacture Philadelphia Cream Cheese in plant here. • Grasslands holds Second International Steeplechase and Glangesia is winner before ten thousand spectators. The King of Spain again furnished a gold cup for the winner. • Brown Milling Company begins producing flour and cornmeal on northeast side of L&N Railroad at Gray Street. • Motorcade celebrates final completion of Jackson Highway.

1932 Grasslands fails. Court appoints receivers. Numerous Gallatin creditors sustain crippling losses. • High school building and Howard Elementary are completed and occupied. • New airport stages night air show. • Interurban ceases operations after twenty years of service between Gallatin and Nashville. • Grassland properties will be sold at public auction.

1933 Depression triggers bank holidays first called by Governor Hill McAlister and next by President Franklin D. Roosevelt, but when local banks reopen, it is business as usual. • Mass meeting at courthouse adopts resolutions in support of President Roosevelt. • City struggles to meet funding requirements for city school system; pay teachers only 75 percent of agreed salaries. • Sale of beer legalized in Gallatin. • Tobacco prizing barn on Red River near the railroad burns. • Jarman Shoe Company of Nashville announces it will locate its first branch manufacturing operation here in former high school building (the Fletcher Hotel building)

A Time Line History Celebrating the Bicentennial of Gallatin, Tennessee

on East Main Street. Remodeling work on structure begins. • Fire damages Foxland Hall on Nashville Pike at Douglass Bend Road. • President Roosevelt appoints *Sumner County News* publisher Edward Albright as minister of the United States to Finland. Albright sells newspaper to Rufus and Elizabeth Boddie. • Federal grant and loan may enable city to put in sewer system throughout entire town. • Merchants sign National Recovery Administration (NRA) agreement with federal government, but NRA will be declared unconstitutional by U.S. Supreme Court within two years. • Congress establishes Tennessee Valley Authority.

1934 City Council votes to pay one-half the cost of an eight-inch sewer line 1,275 feet long from Union High School on Winchester Street to the main trunk line near the junction of Boyers and Smith Streets. As Union is a county school, the county will pay the other one-half. • City awards construction contract for replacement of the standpipe, a vital component of the waterworks system. The old one had rusted out. • Dry gray-brown clouds from Great Plains dust bowl cover eastern United States including Gallatin where humidity level drops to 16 percent. • Health officer says selling and eating watermelons on the Public Square has created a need for waste containers to hold the rinds. • Voters favor sewer system improvement plan in referendum 263 to 116. • City Council sets wage rates. City will pay at thirty cents per hour for unskilled workers and forty cents per hour for skilled labor. • Police force

has two full-time employees, the marshal and assistant marshal. From time to time there are "extra night police."

1935 Local mass meeting instructs state senator and representatives to vote against proposed retail sales tax. • Huge Ford tri-motor airplane is at Gallatin Airport for three days; will provide twelve-mile rides over the city for interested citizens. • Chamber of Commerce promotes Federal Housing Administration loans for residential improvements and repairs. • Eight hundred seven homing pigeons released for flight to Buffalo,

New York, from whence they had been shipped to Gallatin. Large crowd attended the flyaway. • Local editor laments that although the Sumner County Colored Fair Association had annually produced an agricultural fair, the white community had not staged one for ten years. • Air circus entertains with planes, stunt pilots, and parachutists on Erskine Turner farm northeast of town. • Fire destroys a dry kiln at Durham Manufacturing Company. • American Legion Post No. 17 seeks to promote local interest in having Veterans Administration select Gallatin as the site of a new regional hospital.

Courtesy of Sumner County *News*

W. N. Lackey cartoon of the Fletcher Hotel, partially completed and abandoned.

GALLATIN 200

1936 Local Business and Professional Women's Club organizes. • City learns that Veterans Administration hospital will not be located here. • Chamber of Commerce and city and county complete negotiations with Jarman Shoe Company to build a new factory on Factory Lane for the manufacture of shoes. It would be Jarman's second plant in Gallatin. In referendum, citizens vote 657 to 9 to issue bonds to finance part of construction costs. • Large crowd witnesses release of 763 birds for second annual marathon race of homing pigeons to Buffalo, New York. • County court squabbles with state over personnel issues at Sumner County Health Department. Health Department closes. • R. C. Owen Tobacco Company purchases the Owen Tobacco Works of Eagleville founded fifty years earlier by U. J. Owen. Stock and equipment and operations will be moved to Gallatin. • Young Men's Business Club suggests organization of a local country club. • County yields to state and creates a County Board of Health; Health Department will reopen within a few weeks. • The weekly *Examiner-Tennessean* is sold by J. P. Branch to Dan Minnich and Tom Reimer of Havre, Montana, who later sell to E. P. Turner. • Federal Works Progress Administration (WPA) contributes to local health by building sanitary pit toilets and by draining pools along the course of Town Creek to eliminate breeding locales for mosquitoes. • Union High School football team, the Red Devils, conclude season undefeated.

1937 Warehousemen expect million dollars in tobacco sales from 4 to 5 million pound crop. • Merchants split on new courthouse location. • Gallatin High School accreditation drops because of inadequate salary levels. • Crescent Amusement Company of Nashville builds and opens the Roxy, a new motion picture theater, on Nelle Houston Brown property just off the Square on East Main Street. • The President's Ball, a gala to benefit Sumner County crippled children, is held at Gallatin High School. Francis Craig and his Hermitage Hotel WSM-NBC orchestra play for dancing. • New shoe factory building is completed and dedicated; machinery will arrive soon. • Present minister to Finland, Edward Albright, is appointed minister to Costa Rica, but dies eight weeks later. • Cold storage locker system is installed and opens in new building at Sumner County Cooperative Creamery. • Lions International organizes Gallatin club. • Pigeons depart for homing flight to Buffalo, New York. • Citizens in referendum vote for bond issue of $150,000 to buy the existing system from Kentucky-Tennessee Light and Power or build a new city-owned electric distribution system as soon as TVA electricity is available. • Sumner County celebrates its Sesquicentennial with pageant, parade, and

Last spike is driven in Interurban track, 1913.

Courtesy of Allen Haynes Collection

A Time Line History Celebrating the Bicentennial of Gallatin, Tennessee

other public events, all in Gallatin. The parade is attended by fifteen thousand.

1938 Gallatin leases the swimming pool and grounds on Town Creek from E. B. Craig; plans recreation ground, park, tennis courts, horseshoe pits, and band concert stand. • City breaks ground for first sewage treatment plant. • County Court proposes to build new courthouse; referendum on bond issue needed to fund construction passes and demolition of the courthouse of 1837 begins. • City Health Officer Dr. W. N. Lackey urges citizens to clean their premises, to take proper vaccinations, and to keep hogs down on the farm and away from town. • City Council authorizes police station to be open twenty-four hours each day; previously it had been closed at night. • Airmail plane makes first pickup of Gallatin outbound mail from Gallatin Airport. • City accepts WPA bid to build sewage system and disposal plant. • Last minute efforts to build courthouse in a new location off the Public Square fail.

1939 City and Kentucky-Tennessee Light and Power agree on terms of sale of power plant and system to city for $150,000. Title is transferred March 1. • City extends white way (street lighting) about one mile out North and South Water and East and West Main Streets. • A candy factory, Dixie Candy Company, opens here making twenty different kinds of candy. • City signs TVA contract for electric power; citizens can expect a 30 to 40 percent reduction in their monthly electric bills. • Fire destroys Ed Mac Restaurant on Red River Road.

1940 New courthouse on Public Square is dedicated, occupied, and in use. • Severe cold has Cumberland River here frozen over from bank to bank in February. • Barrel staves manufacturer sets up mill on corner of Blythe and Fort Streets. • New Gallatin Aviation Club purchases "cub" airplane. • Newly-arrived tailor put out of Allen's Restaurant at gunpoint for brazenly praising the German Nazi dictator Adolph Hitler. • WPA project enables city to pave nearly all streets not hitherto paved. • Males in the age bracket of twenty-one to twenty-five years register for possible military service. • City population is 4,829.

Courtesy of Crutcher Studio

"Chippy" Drane, Spanish American War veteran.

1942–1944
THE MANEUVERS

From the latter part of 1942 into the spring of 1944, the Second Army conducted training maneuvers in the Gallatin area preparatory to the invasion of Europe. Thousands of young soldiers crowded the town, and citizens welcomed many into their homes for meals or a moment of rest. The maneuver period was an exciting time for Gallatin as troop trains disgorged battle-equipped fighting men at the L&N station and combat tanks and artillery rumbled through town.

Encamped in a large pasture on the Rose Mont farm, Gen. George S. Patton learned that a few enlisted soldiers were paying the owner's daughter-in-law, Mrs. Joan Guild, to do their laundry and sent an orderly to ask the price. Complaining that the charge was too high, Patton sent the orderly back to negotiate. Mrs. Guild responded that if he wanted his clothes washed, he would pay her the same as she charged his soldiers. And he did.

GALLATIN 200

1941 Mercury Development Company proposes airmail service to Gallatin. Mailbag or bags will be dropped from aircraft in flight which will then lower a cable hook to pick up outgoing mailbag on the ground. • River steamer *Idlewild* announces moonlight excursions from Cairo Landing. • Mrs. T. C. Worth, English refugee, leaves her two children here in the care of friends and returns to London. • General Shoe Corporation will have public open house at both of its Gallatin plants that together employ one thousand persons. • Bill Bancroft and Louis M. Starr purchase Gallatin *Examiner*. • Spirited Chamber of Commerce meeting rejects proposal to join National Chamber of Commerce because it had opposed TVA and the South's fight for equal freight rates. • On December 7 Japanese bomb Pearl Harbor and sink key battleships and cruisers of U.S. Pacific Fleet. • United States declares war against Japan.

1942 Wreckers raze L&N Depot Tower of 1858. • Gallatin wakes up to World War II. • City experiences first practice "blackout" as local civil defense girds for action. • First wartime conscription registration is held for men ages twenty to forty-five. • The Second Army will conduct training maneuvers in Gallatin area and moves its headquarters in. • Thousands of troops inundate the town; olive drab jeeps and field cars clog the Square. Gallatin considers Recreation Centers, entertainment for soldiers here on maneuvers.

1943 Farmers quickly rally to mobilize for war production. • Paratroopers' descent startles farmers as soldiers arrive by air and land for second year of training maneuvers. • City will erect bathhouse for soldiers. • Second Army

Architect's rendering of Fletcher Hotel, later a high school, and afterward a General Shoe plant.

Courtesy of Allen Haynes Collection

64

A Time Line History Celebrating the Bicentennial of Gallatin, Tennessee

1944
MANEUVERS END

It may be that the farmers whose fences are flat and the boys who have lived in the rain and mud are glad that the maneuvers of Middle Tennessee are over. The boys have been Catholic, Protestant and Jew, but as they have come into our homes and hearts, there has been no difference between them. With but very, very few exceptions, they have been great boys. Their constant presence in our churches has been a real inspiration to all of us. The ideals for which they are fighting truly live in their hearts. As the boys in uniform leave us, the people of our town say, "Bon Voyage," and with them goes the convoy of our prayers. The Christian people of our churches can truthfully say that we are not glad to see the boys in uniform leave.

—First Methodist Church *Bulletin*, March 26, 1944

chooses area for training because lay of the land and stream patterns are much like the geography of Western Europe. • Exercises marred by soldiers' deaths when army tanks tilt off pontoon bridge while crossing the Cumberland River. • Infantry Gen. George S. Patton camps in field near Rose Mont. • Maneuvers are terminated by late autumn. • Gallatin *Examiner* editor declares that a Cumberland River bridge should be the town's postwar priority. • High School

yearbook, facing shortage of slick paper and binding materials, is printed in newspaper format on newsprint. • Local newspapers print much news from men and women in military service; relate battle experiences.

1944 State Highway Department plans to make four-lane road of Nashville Pike all the way between Gallatin and Nashville. • Fire consumes grandstands on Sumner County Colored Fair Association

grounds. • United States troops lead allied invasion of Europe; thousands had been trained here. • Chamber of Commerce endorses airport for Gallatin. • Ralph Wheatley purchases Gallatin *Examiner.*

1945 City receives grant of five hundred dollars for preliminary airport survey. • City Council sees need for swimming pool, park, tennis courts. • Commonwealth Fund of New York

1945
THE END OF WORLD WAR II

When President Truman announced that World War II had ended with Japan's unconditional surrender, it took only a few moments for Gallatin to come alive. Most people were at home eating dinner. The bell at the fire hall was rung. Owen's Tobacco Factory whistle blew, sirens on the fire engines and horns sounded, and people rushed downtown.

It seemed that people and cars were racing madly around the square. Firecrackers were set off until late night. Pedestrians were afraid to walk down the street and small children were frightened by the noise.

All of the Gallatin churches were opened after the official announcement and many people went for prayer.

Cars seemed to come from every angle—people who had been saving gas now drove up and down streets, blowing their horns. The double header softball game was called off and players were downtown still wearing their uniforms.

—Gallatin *Examiner,*
August 17, 1945

GALLATIN 200

City grants seventy-five thousand dollars for construction of a public health center at Gallatin. City and county will furnish the site on southeast corner of Winchester and South Water Streets. • Readers of local newspapers pore over news from men and women in military service. • School children mobilize in biggest salvage campaign in history of the state. • Council votes 4 to 3 to keep beer in Gallatin. • Palace Theater is damaged by fire. • City Council regulates beer taverns; bans booths and high back chairs—"a tough break for the smoochers." • The General Shoe Corporation announces it has signed contract with U.S. government to manufacture and supply approximately one million pairs of combat boots and service shoes for the Army. • President Franklin Roosevelt dies and Vice President Harry Truman succeeds him. • Legion Post No. 17 wants to construct a building, "a living memorial to Sumner County men and women who died" in World Wars I and II, for the use of ex-servicemen. • City celebrates VE (Victory in Europe) Day. Church bells ring and citizens gather to pray. Celebration was muted by realization that the war in Asia still raged. • Windstorm with hurricane force winds cuts path of destruction through Gallatin from Peytona to Bethpage. • City Council votes against leasing Sullivan farm for airport because lease rate of twenty-five hundred dollars per year was regarded as excessive. Council will call for a referendum to authorize purchase of an airport site and construction of the necessary improvements upon it. • Additions to local cheese plant make it the largest of its kind in the South. It will employ 110 persons. • Japan surrenders to Allies ending Pacific and Asian War and town goes wild with

Gallatin Church of Christ, East Main.

By Allen Haynes

A Time Line History Celebrating the Bicentennial of Gallatin, Tennessee

joy. • R. C. Owen Tobacco Company plant is hit by one hundred thousand dollar fire. • City votes to purchase site on Morrison Street for city park and site of a second water tank.

1946 Town Creek rampages, biggest flood in history of Gallatin; much property damage. • Lions Club presents minstrel show that becomes annual event. • Largest downtown crowd since Sesquicentennial of 1937 attends opening of new automobile dealership Wade Motor Company in new building on West Main Street. • Community cannery is open one day each week. • R. C. Owen Tobacco Company builds modern redrying facility; to open in December. • En route to an air museum in Tucson, Arizona, a German World War II combat plane makes an emergency landing on the Langley Hall farm. • Sumner County Fair Association completing barns and grandstand at new show grounds on West Main Street for first fair since 1927. • Rotary Club funds construction of additional seating at GHS football field. • Sumner County Creamery adds equipment to process whole milk; only had cream capability previously. • In referendum, burley growers countywide favor quotas. • New streamlined railroad train to be routed through Gallatin by end of year. • Fire destroys five adjacent business houses on North Water Street just north of the Palace Theater. • Citizens are interested in aviation rally "to put Gallatin on the aviation map." • General Eisenhower outlines schedule for demobilization.

Citizens Club Calendar.

Courtesy of Sumner County Archives

• City Council votes to install parking meters on Public Square and to purchase new auto to replace the one and only police car. • Veterans of Foreign Wars establish post here. • Jaycees organize local group. • Postwar building boom begins, although materials are in short supply.

1947 The newly completed Cordell Hull Hotel opens on West Main Street. • Students overflow city schools; Howard Elementary uses rooms at Baptist Church next door and in Sumner County Memorial Home a block away. • Fourth annual General Shoe employee picnic attracts crowd of thirty-five hundred. • A

GALLATIN 200

1947
RANDY'S RECORD SHOP

In 1947 Randy's Record Shop began selling records by mail order, collect on delivery. Advertising over the powerful Nashville radio station WLAC, Randy's message could be heard throughout most of the southeastern United States.

Within two or three years, the shop was inundated with mail orders and shipped such a heavy volume that it resulted in an upgrade of the local post office.

An unintended consequence of the advertising was the attention it focused on "Gallatin, Tennessee," mentioned emphatically in every repetition of Randy's mailing address. For the next decade, Gallatin became known to hundreds of thousands in the Southeast as the home of Randy's Record Shop.

retail furniture store located on South Water Street, predecessor to Cresent Manufacturing Company, is incorporated by local investors Charles R. Tomkins Jr. and Charles Fowler. • Local men receive permit to operate new radio station WHIN on AM frequencies. • Fire guts three stores: a barbershop, a dry goods store, and a restaurant on the west side of North Water Street in remodeled Jones Livery Company building. • General Assembly passes bill to build bridge at Woods Ferry, but Governor Jim McCord vetoes it. • Gallatin experiences picketing by labor union for first time in strike by employees of Southern Bell Telephone and Telegraph Company. • Preparation for first city-owned public park is underway on nine-acre tract on Morrison Street. • Last of World War II rationing is terminated. • Privately owned buses begin operation within the city. • Union High School band tours Midwest as far north as Detroit. • Sumner County Health Department moves into new building on South Water Street. • County acquires land just east of North Water Street for new elementary school that will be named for the beloved teacher Vena Stuart. • Building contractors complete Lambuth Methodist Church on South Water, several new business houses, and a burley tobacco sales floor. • Randy's Record Shop begins advertising mail order sales over WLAC radio, Nashville.

1948 H. E. Franklin and Sons Machine Shop on East Franklin will begin manufacturing truck bodies designed for hauling milk. • National Stores has grand opening for adjoining department and hardware stores. • City Council calls for referendum on issues of daylight savings time and Sunday movies. • Gallatin Country Club organizes. • Civic clubs begin drive to fund public swimming pool construction. • Fire damages three commercial buildings on Red River

Cumberland Telephone Building of 1922.

Courtesy of Allen Haynes Collection

A Time Line History Celebrating the Bicentennial of Gallatin, Tennessee

and explodes fireworks stored in another on North Water. • Congressman Albert Gore Sr. addresses Armistice Day gathering. • Members of First Baptist Church on East Main vote to raze old sanctuary, build a larger one, and enlarge the educational building. • New addition to Sumner Creamery enables production of both condensed and dry milk. Plant will continue to manufacture Blue Grass Butter. • Improvements are made to facilities at Gallatin High School. • Radio station WHIN begins broadcasting. • Voters in referendum approve seven hundred thousand dollar bond issue to finance natural gas distribution system. • Parochial school opens at St. John's Vianney on North Water Street. • Gallatin Country Club is organized; buys property on Scottsville Pike for clubhouse, golf course, and other facilities. • Fast growing mail-order sales prompt Randy's Record Shop move to new West Main Street location. • City Council purchases eight-acre tract for Clearview Park. • Kraft Foods completes plant addition for laboratory and warehouse.

1949 Roof structure of Rose Mont, home of Judge and Mrs. Lewis Guild, gutted by fire. • Governor Gordon Browning signs bill to build bridge across Cumberland River at Woods Ferry. • County will erect new building for Union High School. • City Council votes ten thousand dollars to partially fund public swimming pool; additional funds needed. • General Shoe sponsors safety rally with parade and other entertainment, attracts crowd believed to be largest ever in town. • Alexander Funeral Home moves into new facility at corner of West Main and Foster Streets.

1950 Mississippi Vocational College is founded at Itta Bena by James Hubert White, an African American formerly of Gallatin. He was president of the college from

First Union High School.

Courtesy of Velma Brinkley Collection

GALLATIN 200

1952
YALE AND TOWNE

Yale and Towne Manufacturing Company not only made Gallatin the principal source of Yale locks for several years, but conducted a training program for tool and die makers that may have been its greatest local legacy. Some of the trainee graduates have had their own tool and die shops in Gallatin for thirty years or more. Together they employ a substantial number of skilled workers and conduct business throughout the United States.

1950 until he retired in 1971. • Plans revealed for a National Guard Armory to be built here. • Cumberland River bridge construction contract is awarded. • Gallatin Country Club golf course is ready for play; construction of clubhouse begins. • New swimming pool is open at E.W. Thompson City Park. • Local men see action in outbreak of Korean War; draft board makes first call for that war. • Local National Guard company is called to active duty. • Chamber of Commerce meeting discusses impact of proposed high dam on Cumberland near Hendersonville and the lake it will create. • City accepts separate bids to extend sewer lines and to install natural gas distribution system. • A handful of television sets receive first television transmissions from a Nashville station. • Population is 5,107.

1951 Dr. Robert N. Moore opens Robert Moore General Hospital on East Main Street. • New Union High School opens; school buses will transport black students from all parts of county to Union. • "The worst ice, sleet, and snowstorm in the history of Sumner County" paralyzes city late in the evening of January 31. • Popular pastor laments neglect of rental housing and asks city to use its authority to enforce standard specifications that would render quarters acceptable for human habitation. • Fire guts Gallatin High School building as extensive remodeling neared completion. • Local Industrial Development Association formed to seek additional industry. • Estes Kefauver for President club formed here.

1952 Natural gas turned on in newly installed system. • Johnny Maddox begins first tour of theaters and clubs as piano entertainer building on his nationwide recording popularity on Dot Records. • First public housing units for Gallatin receive federal approval. • Industrial Development Association announces that the Yale and Towne Manufacturing Company of Stamford, Connecticut, will build and operate a lock plant here. • TVA proposes to build steam electric generating plant in Coles Bend of the Cumberland River; work to begin next year. • By midsummer there are three thousand telephones on the Gallatin exchange. • Cresent Furniture Store closes here; is reopened in Nashville as Cresent Wholesale. Owners purchase furniture manufacturing plant in Nashville.

1953 Many local men and women are on duty in Korean War; several on the fighting fronts. • Community welcomes Yale and Towne; plant is dedicated. • Loveless Hospital opens on South Water Street; is second private hospital in town. • Building is completed on East Main Street to house Dr. C. D.

Courtesy of Gallatin Chamber of Commerce
Palace Theater.

A Time Line History Celebrating the Bicentennial of Gallatin, Tennessee

Courtesy of Sumner County Archives

Interurban car and crew.

Giles's new medical clinic. • Public schools offer free textbooks for first time. • Ralph Rogers Company opens rock quarry on Odom's Bend Road.

1954 Workers place initial concrete in foundation of TVA steam plant powerhouse. • Cumberland River bridge, called Veterans Memorial, is open to traffic. • Housing authority will plan redevelopment of two slum areas. • UT Extension Service

---

1954
GENERAL SHOE CORPORATION

In 1954 General Shoe employed 817 people in two Gallatin plants with total annual wages of $2,102,727.64. The two operations produced and shipped eighty-four hundred pairs of shoes on each working day.

General Shoe's lifesaving contribution to Gallatin was providing regular work and a dependable payroll during the depths of the Great Depression when getting any kind of job was not easy.

One of the three founders of the company in 1924 was William H. Wemyss of Gallatin. Sarah Mac Anderson of Gallatin was the wife of Maxey Jarman, son of founder James Franklin Jarman and his father's successor in the company in 1938. The third founder, J. H. Lawson, lived in Hendersonville.

71

promotes organization of county community clubs. • The Cresent Manufacturing Company announces plans to move its furniture-making plant here from Nashville and will locate it on Maple Street. • Corps of Engineers begins impounding Old Hickory Lake.

1955 City approves Industrial Development Committee's request for construction of a factory building for a garment manufacturer; prospective employees file two thousand job applications. • Town Creek redevelopment plans are approved; federal aid for slum clearance is forthcoming. • Cumberland Electric Membership Corporation, a rural electric cooperative, dedicates new headquarters building and storage yard at corner of Blythe Street and Highway 109. • Ellis Jones's FM radio station WFMG begins broadcasting.

1956 Local burley leaf sales market rates fourth largest in state. • Interest grows for hospital, publicly owned and operated. • City Council votes to redevelop 32.6 acres in Town Creek area. • Purchased by Paramount Records, Dot Records moves to Los Angeles to a location on corner of Sunset Boulevard at Vine. Randy's Record Shop remains here, but Randy Wood goes to Los Angeles. • First two generators begin power production at TVA Steam Plant; construction begins on units 3 and 4. •

Courtesy of Allen Haynes Collection
A Big Cheese at Kraft Foods.

By Walter T. Durham
This concrete and steel building erected in 1927 by J. A. Sloan and Company housed the wholesale grocery operations of Charles C. Parks Company until 1979 when Parks relocated to a modern, more accessible facility on Belvedere Drive. During the last twenty years, the Depot Square Shopping Center, and more recently, the manufacturing and distribution operations of Volunteer Box have occupied the former grocery warehouse.

New Guild Elementary School is completed, dedicated, and opened on South Water Street.

1957 New Byron's Bar-B-Q opens plant; produces frozen barbecue and related products. • The Corps of Engineers dedicates Old Hickory Dam on Cumberland near Hendersonville. • Fire destroys Crescent Amusement Company's Roxy Theater on East Main just off the square. • Public attention is focused on industrial and economic development. • Ralph Rogers Company begins producing asphalt paving mix at quarry location on Odom's Bend Road.

1958 The Gallatin Aluminum Products Company, Inc., purchases thirteen acres on Maple Street and builds twenty thousand square foot plant.

A Time Line History Celebrating the Bicentennial of Gallatin, Tennessee

1959 Year-long negotiations for a plant location for a Detroit cutting tool manufacturer are broken off with no results. • Middle Tennessee Council Boy Scouts of America announces plans to develop Camp Boxwell across the lake from Gallatin. • Locals participate in active oil and gas leasing throughout upper parts of county. • Houseboat manufacturing begins here at Kop Ron Machine Company. • TVA puts power generating units 3 and 4 into operation at Gallatin Steam Plant. • New Sumner County Memorial Hospital opens; facility built with financial assistance from federal Hill-Burton Act. • Housing Authority applies for funding for seventy-five more housing units. • Corps of Engineers expects four million visitors to Old Hickory Lake this year; had three million last year.

Courtesy of Allen Haynes Collection

Woods Ferry.

1960 Gallatin loses to Murfreesboro in competition for plant to manufacture Samsonite travel products. • Gallatin Aluminum adds thirty thousand square feet to plant floor space. •

Courtesy of Sumner County Archives

Grasslands finish line.

73

GALLATIN 200

Courthouse of 1837, photo circa 1930.

Trojan Homes begins manufacture of mobile homes at Long Hollow plant site. • Kraft Foods and Sumner Creamery purchased milk from Sumner Farmers last year in the amount of $1,285,816. • Census shows city population to be 7,857. • Telephone company switches all phones to dial system. • Ellis Jones's AM radio station WAMG begins broadcasting. • Voters approve county industrial revenue bond issue to construct plant for Dominion Electric Company; factory is in limited operation by mid-December. • Broadway bypass highway construction is begun through Town Creek redevelopment area. • City population is 7,901. • *Upper Sumner Press* is consolidated with Gallatin *Examiner* which was acquired earlier by the James E. Charlet publishing interests.

1961 County Board of Education moves into new building on Winchester Street. • Hamilton-Cosco, Inc., announces office furniture plant for Gallatin; will erect factory building of 211,000 square feet. • County Court

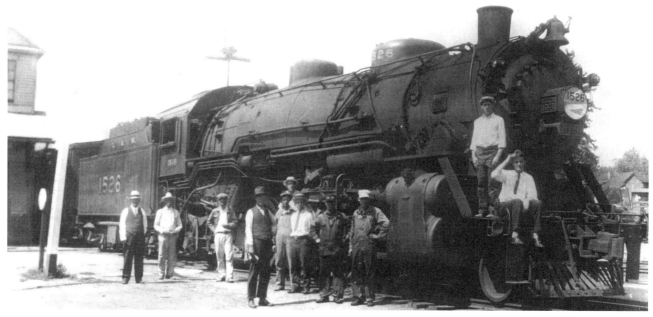

L&N Steam Locomotive at depot about 1930.

A Time Line History Celebrating the Bicentennial of Gallatin, Tennessee

Courtesy of Allen Haynes Collection

Gallatin High School of 1932.

Courtesy of Allen Haynes Collection

Gallatin High School of 1932 with later additions.

approves plans for construction of county airport at Gallatin; awaits federal funds. • Citizens look to fallout shelters for protection against nuclear bomb attack. • Cresent Manufacturing adds six thousand square feet to plant; will add forty employees. • Successor to the original shirt manufacturer, the Gary Company expands plant by 29,200 square feet. Expects to add 150 employees to present level of 285. • Local merchants report record Christmas sales.

1962 Employment at Shaffer Corporation, the local division of Dominion Electric, is at 425 persons. Company will add fifty thosuand square feet to plant area. • Civitan plans to organize club here. • Sumner schoolteachers' salaries are below that of all adjacent counties and far below state average. • County purchases 162 acres on Cairo Road for airport. • City plans to extend services and increase pumping capacity at water plant. • Ralph Rogers Company purchases Pilot Knob Hill and begins mining stone from inside the large limestone knob. • Kraft Foods acquires two acres adjoining the plant for expansion of facility. • Fire guts top (third) floor of Genesco shoe plant on East Main Street and damages building throughout. Company will restore the building and resume manufacturing. • A large confused deer leaps through plate glass window of Hotel Cordell Hull into lobby. • Local public supports President John F. Kennedy's crackdown on Russian missiles in Cuba; many consider building bomb shelters.

General Shoe Corporation, formerly the Fletcher Hotel.

Courtesy of Allen Haynes Collection

R. C. Owen Company Office Building.

By Allen Haynes

A Time Line History Celebrating the Bicentennial of Gallatin, Tennessee

By Allen Haynes

Sumner County Courthouse.

1963 Cosco begins production of metal office furniture. • Genesco plant on East Main returns to full operation after fire last year. • Ralph Rogers Company begins producing asphalt paving mix at Pilot Knob location. • Gallatin Aluminum will add thirty thousand square feet of manufacturing space. • Genesco workers vote against representation by labor union. • Yale and Towne to add twenty-six thousand square feet to plant and sixty new jobs. • Renewed phospate mining north of town sends about eighteen railroad carloads per day to processing plants located outside the county. • District attorney brings ouster suit against mayor charged with buying city supplies from his own store. •

Roxy Theater.

Courtesy of Allen Haynes Collection

77

Gallatin 200

Courthouse dedication, 1941.

Courtesy of Walter T. Durham Collection

Training maneuvers pontoon bridge, World War II.

Courtesy of Sumner County Archives

Airport is ready for business. • *Sumner County News* is purchased by owners of Gallatin *Examiner*.

1964 Governor Frank Clement chooses Public Square to launch race for U.S. Senate. • Per capita income in Sumner County is nearly double that of ten years ago. • Voters approve $320,000 industrial revenue bonds for Gallatin Aluminum; will enlarge plant by fifty thousand square feet. • Officials dedicate newly completed Gallatin Junior High School on Scottsville Pike. • Council votes to extend water mains sixty-three thousand linear feet. • U.S. Postal Service authorizes major repairs to post office on East Main Street.

1965 School Board votes to comply with state

A Time Line History Celebrating the Bicentennial of Gallatin, Tennessee

guidelines to the Civil Rights Act of 1964. • Head Start program begins for preschoolers. • Yale and Towne workers participate in three-day wildcat strike. • Shaffer employees choose to be represented by Machinists Union. • Carpenters and Joiners Union strikes at Cosco. • Community is participating in first Adult Basic Education Program. • State extends Highway 109 southward from U.S. Highway 70 to Interstate 40.

1966 Genesco workers vote against union representation 459 to 293. • A new public library building is under construction on Hartsville Pike. • Voting machines used for first time here in November 8 election. • Grocers

Courtesy of Allen Haynes Collection
Farmers and military observers watch paratroopers' descent during training maneuvers here.

By Allen Haynes

Barge traffic beneath Cumberland River Bridge on State Highway 109.

79

Gallatin 200

Impromptu Unity Day.

Courtesy of Velma Brinkley Collection

Twister at work at R. C. Owen Company.

By Allen Haynes

learn procedures for handling food stamps under new Federal Food Stamp Program. • Department of Electricity builds offices and warehouse on Jones Street.

1967 Wildcat strike leads to Shaffer decision to close plant here and switch its production elsewhere. • City sells Shaffer building to Genesco for use as warehouse and distribution point. • Gary Company employees reject unionization by a vote margin of four to one. • City voters approve package liquor stores by vote of 1,392 to 1,387.

1968 Fighting in Vietnam is increasing; local soldiers die in combat. • Through his

A Time Line History Celebrating the Bicentennial of Gallatin, Tennessee

By Allen Haynes

Sumner County Fair chooses Fairest of the Fair.

By Allen Haynes

Sumner County Fair midway lights up at night.

new company, Ran-Wood Production, Randy Wood contracts to release and distribute all future music recordings for the nationally renowned entertainer and orchestra leader Lawrence Welk. • Although Sumner Board of Education had complied with state guidelines about segregated schools, the results are not satisfactory to the federal enforcing authority. Sumner is ordered to integrate students and faculty by beginning of school year 1969–1970. • Ground is broken for building to house Tennessee Vocational Training Center for mentally retarded and physically handicapped. • Local African Americans organize the Sumner County branch of the National Association for the Advancement of Colored People.

1969 United States sends a man to a soft landing on the moon and returns him home safely. • Public library construction is finished and library is named for Edward Ward Carmack, native Sumner Countian who was later a U.S. Congressman, Senator, and politically active newspaper publisher. • Gallatin Boat Works, Inc., completes nine thousand square foot plant to build steel hull houseboats. • Sumner County Hospital announces plans to build an addition estimated to cost $2.2 million. • L&N passenger and freight depot, parts of which were built about 1858, is demolished by railroad company. • Effective local lobbying for a junior college results in state announcement of location of Volunteer State Community College on one hundred acres on Nashville Pike. • Hamilton Cosco plans to add seventy thousand square foot floor area to plant.

1970 Federal agency threatens to sue Sumner County Board of Education for failure to integrate schools but will allow additional time if good faith effort is made. • Construction of college will begin this autumn. Dr. Hal R. Ramer is named its first president. • State chooses 142 acres on Bledsoe Creek to make improvements so that it can be used as a park for campers. • City population is 13,093.

1971 Citizens group proposes change to strong mayor type of city government. • Blaze damages Cresent Manufacturing Company plant and is confined to finishing room. • Facilities for General Sessions Court, the sheriff's office, and county jail are under construction on southwest corner of Smith Street and South Water. • Farm Bureau opens headquarters in new building at 400 North Boyers Avenue. • Volunteer State Community College begins first classes. • Construction begins on twenty-five

Union High School of 1949.

Courtesy of Velma Brinkley Collection

A Time Line History Celebrating the Bicentennial of Gallatin, Tennessee

By Allen Haynes

The church of 1950, First Baptist, East Main.

thousand square foot plant on Pumping Station Road for Watercraft to build houseboats. • Martha White Industries of Nashville, later acquired by Beatrice Foods, buys locally owned Byron's Bar-B-Q, pioneer producer of frozen barbecue products.

1972 The Sumner County Guidance Center opens here. • County accepts bids to construct new Gallatin High School. • Gary Company breaks ground on another plant addition. • Gallatin and Hendersonville hassle over Gallatin's west side annexation plans. • Locally owned Gallatin Aluminum Products Company, Inc. (GAPCO), with payroll of 388 employees, is purchased by Redman Building Products, a division of Redman Industries of Dallas, Texas. • Construction of quarters for the General Sessions Court, the sheriff's office, and the county jail is finished. • The city purchases sixty-five acres one mile north of Public Square for municipal park. • DORCO opens to manufacture storm windows and doors.

1973 *News-Examiner* sells to Multimedia, Inc., of Greenville, South Carolina. • Citizens learn that TVA may locate a nuclear powered electric generating plant near Hartsville and assess impact on Gallatin. • Locally owned Sumner County Bank and Trust Company is purchased by First Tennessee Bank of Memphis. • GAPCO employees vote for representation by Teamsters Union. After a yearlong strike, employees vote to decertify the union. • A new private school, Sumner Academy, will open this fall on Nashville Pike for first through sixth grades. By 2001 it will add the seventh and eighth grades, pre-kindergarten and kindergarten and move to a new campus on Nichols Lane. • R. R. Donnelley and Sons, the world's largest independent printer, becomes newest member of local industrial community. Large state-of-the-art printing plant is under construction on Steam Plant Road. • Gallatin Senior High School men's basketball team wins state championship.

Yale and Towne Manufacturing Company. Courtesy of Walter T. Durham Collection

1974 The Gallatin Police Department hires first policewoman. • Contract to construct new City Hall and separate fire headquarters is awarded to low bidder. The City Hall, located on West Main Street near the Public Square, will have thirty thousand square feet of office space plus a kitchen and dining room for public events. The spacious fire headquarters is nearby at corner of Foster and West Franklin Streets. • Corps of Engineers approves seaplane operations on Old Hickory Lake on trial basis for twelve months. • TVA applies to Atomic Energy Commission for approval of plans to build nuclear power plant at Hartsville. • Genesco closes East Main Street shoe factory; shifts production to Factory Lane plant.

1975 Local jobless rate is 7 percent, about the same as in adjacent counties. • Environmental Protection Agency grants funds to city for study of three-part sewage improvement project. • County erects new building for vocational education at Gallatin

Randy's Record Shop as shown on catalog cover. Courtesy of Allen Haynes Collection

A Time Line History Celebrating the Bicentennial of Gallatin, Tennessee

Courtesy of Gallatin Chamber of Commerce

Welcome to Gallatin!

Senior High School. • History buffs organize Sumner County Historical Society. • Illegal drug traffic continues its long run. Police raids collect guns, cash, and drugs, but the traffic survives. • Officials dedicate new City Hall and fire headquarters.

1976 The former Watercraft plant is now occupied by the industrial systems division of the Ferro Corporation. • TVA begins construction of massive nuclear-powered electric generating plant at Hartsville and expects five hundred construction workers to move into Sumner County. • Financing is approved for Christian Towers, Inc., a locally organized not-for-profit corporation, to build one hundred housing units for the elderly on East Franklin Street. • TVA

1975
R. R. DONNELLEY & SONS

The Gallatin Division of R. R. Donnelley & Sons will celebrate twenty-seven years of successful operations in 2002. Over the years, the plant has produced a multitude of different magazines, catalogs, and newspaper inserts and has evolved into a premier printer of weekly magazines and retail inserts.

Donnelley and its employees have been very involved in the growth of our community. Instrumental in the creation of the Sumner County United Way in 1977, Donnelley has since received the United Way's Gold Achievement Award for Giving every year. The company contributed a significant grant to Temporary Residence for Adolescents in Crisis, Inc. to build its group home in Gallatin and has financed several historical highway markers to recognize minorities and their achievements.

Gallatin 200

TVA Gallatin Fossil Plant Powerhouse, Units 1 and 2 during construction.

Courtesy of Tennessee Valley Authority

installs four combustion turbines at Gallatin Steam Plant that will burn either natural gas or fuel oil. • DORCO organizes sister company ESP to manufacture insulated window products. • City sells Genesco plant property on East Main at auction to First Baptist Church for ninety-one thousand dollars. • Private property owner requests and receives zoning for four hundred-acre industrial park on east side of town.

1977 Eaton Corporation consolidates all of its brake manufacturing here in former Yale and Towne plant; switches lock and hardware production to another location. • Globe Business Furniture,

TVA Gallatin Fossil Plant, Units 3 and 4 during construction.

Courtesy of Tennessee Valley Authority

the successor to Hamilton-Cosco, will relocate to Hendersonville, and the vacated building will be occupied for office furniture manufacturing by GF Business Equipment, Inc. • A lightning-ignited blaze destroys a large lumber storage building and its contents at Durham Building Supply. • The Hoeganaes Corporation announces it has chosen Gallatin as the location for a new powdered metals plant. • Ground is broken for the new Howard Elementary School on Long Hollow Pike. • Community discusses a possible river port for Gallatin and the proposal for a "thermal plant" to burn garbage.

Gallatin 200

Courtesy of Cresent Manufacturing Company

The extensive furniture production facility at Cresent Manufacturing Company is shown in the center of this aerial view. It lies on both the north and south sides of Maple Street.

A Time Line History Celebrating the Bicentennial of Gallatin, Tennessee

Gallatin Aluminum Products Company, Inc.

Courtesy of Sumner County Archives

Courtesy of U.S. Corps of Engineers
Catch of the day on Old Hickory Lake.

1978 The L&N Railroad Co. announces plans to abandon rail line from Gallatin to Hartsville. • Byron's employees strike over union recognition issue. • County abandons plans to renovate old Howard School on East Main because of high costs involved. • City and county discuss new terminal for Gallatin Airport. • Gallatin High School graduates 287 students. • County Industrial Board approves $3.35 million bond issue for improvements at Hoeganaes plant; $2.35 million will be used for pollution control. Total investment in plant and equipment reaches $31 million. • Three local newspapers owned by Multimedia, Inc., the *Sumner County News*, the Gallatin *Examiner*, and the Sumner *Times*, merge into a single entity: the Gallatin *Examiner-News*. It will be published three times each week. The name later changed to *News-Examiner*. • County Board of Education builds maintenance facility for school buses on Airport Road. • The Armitage Company will construct an industrial paint plant with seven thousand square feet of floor area at 545 National Drive. • Will-Ro Corporation will build a 12,500 square foot plant at 1155 Old Highway 109 North to manufacture custom designed highway towable trailers. • Locally owned Gemco Electric plant on Airport Road opens to manufacture loud speakers and devices for the wired distribution of sound. • Detroit Aluminum Brass, operating as DAB Industries plans to manufacture auto bearings and related parts in new plant to be located on North Belvedere. • Gallatin Block Company begins construction of $1.5 million dollar plant on Station

89

GALLATIN 200

Sailboat on Old Hickory Lake.

Courtesy of U.S. Corps of Engineers

A Time Line History Celebrating the Bicentennial of Gallatin, Tennessee

Camp Creek Road. • Gallatin Senior High School football team wins AAA state championship in Clinic Bowl. • City's slow response to traffic congestion draws fire from *Examiner-News*.

1979 Radio Station WVCP of Volunteer State Community College begins broadcast at 88.3 on the FM dial. • From January 1 through February 21, twenty-five inches of snow fell on Gallatin. • Eaton workers strike over slow progress in contract negotiations. • The governments of Gallatin, Hendersonville, and Sumner County agree to funding plan to build and operate a thermal plant for burning garbage and producing steam and electricity. Sumner Resource Authority created to operate the facility. • R. R. Donnelley will use $10 million industrial revenue bonds to finance acquisition and installation of pollution control system. • TVA reduces plans for nuclear powered generators at Hartsville from four units to two. • City faces $10 million sewer overhaul. • Gallatin Housing Authority receives federal approval to build one hundred new housing units in town just north of Red River Road. • County Commission votes against proposed sale of Sumner Memorial Hospital. • U.S. Department of the Interior declares Fairvue a national historic landmark. • City will receive applications for cable TV franchise. • Fowler Brothers proposes hardwood lumber concentration yard and dry kilns for location on Airport Road. • Local consumers face reduced supplies of gasoline and other petroleum products due to OPEC cutbacks.

1980 Genesco closes Factory Lane shoe plant that had been in operation since 1938 ending a long presence in town. • City leases facility to Acme Boot with promise of three hundred jobs. • Sumner County Museum announces plans to build on Smith Street behind Trousdale Place. • New building set for Clearview Park; other parks will get improvements. • Downtown revitalization costing approximately $7 million is proposed. • July 8 tornado fells trees, topples utility poles and towers; extensive property losses, but no lives lost. • Barbara Mandrell of Gallatin elected Country Music Association Entertainer of the Year. • Separate strikes idle workers at

Courtesy of Gallatin Department of Electricity

Pole replacement, 1960, by linemen who had scaled the pole with climbing hooks.

Charles C. Parks Company and GF Office Furniture. • Sumner Memorial Hospital receives approval from State Health Facilities Commission for $6.34 million expansion. • City population is 17,191.

1981 Citizens rejoice in safe return of U.S. hostages held in Iran. • Western Reserve Plastics of Akron, Ohio, will locate plant on North Belvedere; $750,000 industrial bond issue is approved for the company. • City plans to construct public golf course over the Long Hollow Pike landfill; will be ready for play by August 1982. • Depot Square development is proposed in former wholesale grocery building at the L&N Depot. • Corps of Engineers fine-tunes its lakeshore management plan; invites comments from advisory committee of lakeshore residents. • Annual inflation rate for nation reaches 15.2 percent in July. • Concerned about cost overruns, TVA examines its options for the Hartsville nuclear power plant construction.

1982 TVA halts construction of the nuclear plant at Hartsville; may sell the two reactors originally intended for the facility. • Country music artist Conway Twitty opens Twitty City, a $3.5 million entertainment complex on Nashville Pike just west of Gallatin city limits. • Acme Boot discontinues Gallatin plant operations. • City Council considers acquiring and managing an industrial park. • *News-Examiner* hails thermal plant of Sumner Resource Authority as "a civilized solution to trash," but soot from the fires prompts complaints. • Lake edge residents seek less restrictive boat dock privileges from Corps of Engineers. • Handicapped Adult

By Allen Haynes

Gallatin Department of Electricity headquarters building.

Courtesy of Gallatin Chamber of Commerce

Edward Ward Carmack Public Library.

Training Services at 425 South Water receives state accreditation. • Sumner is seventh most populous county in the state. • Beerless Octoberfest holds forth for three days on Public Square and City Hall parking lot. • Gallatin Green Wave football team loses in prestigious Clinic Bowl game. • Decline in interest rates sparks boom in residential construction.

1983 Would-be developers propose conversion of Foxland Hall's 435 acres into theme park called Country Music World. • Downtown area joins Main Street Program of National Trust for Historic Preservation as one of five pilot projects in Tennessee. • Greater Gallatin, Inc., is organized to revitalize and restore the historic downtown area. • Sumner County Colored Agricultural Fair Association discontinues annual event that has been an important institution for more than

GALLATIN 200

Sumner County General Sessions Court Building. By Allen Haynes

one hundred years. The association will sell fairgrounds on Blythe Street. • Good Neighbor Mission is established on Smith Street. • A nationally acclaimed platform speaker and author of fifty novels, Opie Read dies in Chicago. Early in his career he had been employed by a local printing shop. • Year ends with severe ice storm.

1984 State Department of Transportation plans Gallatin bypass for Highway 109; will swing around west side of town. • Local officials have no interest in Nashville Gas Company's offer to purchase Gallatin Natural Gas System. • Country Music World developers fumble for investors; report that Hank Williams Jr. and Tammy Wynette have signed to participate but furnish no details. A few weeks later CMW sells to an unidentified out-of-town buyer. • GF Office Furniture says will double plant size and add 250 new jobs. • Kraft Foods will close local plant; twenty-eight employees affected. • Three-year-old Depot Square retail

St. John Vianney School of 1950s. By Allen Haynes

A Time Line History Celebrating the Bicentennial of Gallatin, Tennessee

By Allen Haynes

Sumner Academy.

By Allen Haynes

Gallatin Senior High School.

Gallatin 200

R. R. Donnelley & Sons plant.   Courtesy of R. R. Donnelley & Sons Co.

center closes; expected sales did not materialize. • Western Reserve Plastics plans million-dollar expansion as Hoeganaes orders fourth annealing furnace. It will cost $1.75 million. • Village Green proprietors propose residential, office, retail, and personal services development on eighty-five-acre site, most of which was formerly known as the W. J. Fitts property, on north side of Nashville Pike. • Police arrest fifty-seven in drug bust. • Main Post Office will relocate to building just started at corner of Maple Street and Fairground Road. • Voters decide against sale of liquor by the drink. • TRW, Inc., purchases DAB, but will soon sell the North Belvedere plant to Bendix Corporation. • TVA cancels all work on

Skilled worker at R. R. Donnelley & Sons.   Courtesy of R. R. Donnelley & Sons Co.

A Time Line History Celebrating the Bicentennial of Gallatin, Tennessee

By Allen Haynes

Old Hickory Lake vista.

nuclear plant at Hartsville. • State begins construction of a new armory on Hartsville Pike. • Construction of the Municipal Golf Course on Long Hollow Pike progresses slowly.

1985 Severe cold, winds, and snow send temperature to sixteen degrees below zero with wind chill in some local areas at sixty-five degrees below. • Country Music World investors plan to convert from proposed theme park into residential-commercial development. • Formfit Rogers, in bankruptcy, closes local distribution center. • Local man begins manufacture of industrial hoses in start-up operation.

• The National Register of Historic Places accepts Public Square and adjacent area for designation as historic dictrict. • Gallatin Senior High School women's cross-country team wins state championship. • Allied Signal, a division of Bendix Corporation, moves an automotive parts manufacturing plant into the vacant former DAB plant on Belvedere Drive. • A Chicago developer purchases rights to Foxland Hall-Country Music World property and asks for industrial revenue bond issue of $290 million to build apartment complex. • Health, Education, and Housing Facilities Board approves request scaled down to $115 million. • Sunbelt Container, Inc., builds fifty thousand square foot plant at 1440 Airport Road to supply containers for local manufacturers. • The mayor vetoes council approval of Housing Authority application for fifty residential units. • Locals hear Nashville Symphony concert at Cragfont. • Growth of city and county pushes government budgets to record heights. • Sumner Memorial Hospital may be target for private sector purchase. • Westinghouse Corporation offers to become contract manager of thermal plant.

1986 Gallatin Airport opens new terminal building.

Gallatin 200

Downtown Gallatin aerial view, circa 1979.

Courtesy of Allen Haynes Collection

A Time Line History Celebrating the Bicentennial of Gallatin, Tennessee

By Allen Haynes

GF Office Furniture Ltd.

By Allen Haynes

Sumner Resource Authority.

Officials seek federal funds for ILS Navigational System. • Gallatin Aluminum Products Co., Inc., completes addition of fifty thousand square foot floor space. • Citizens join in celebrating statewide Homecoming '86 and the Sumner County Bicentennial. • State gives National Guard Armory on South Water Street jointly to city and county; city wants two hundred thousand dollars for its half interest. • Rebound, a Gallatin-based rehabilitation center for head injury patients, receives national attention for quality care. • Locally owned First and Peoples National Bank is acquired by the First American Corporation of Nashville. It and the former Sumner County Bank and Trust Company are the only two Gallatin banks that can trace their origins to the early years of the twentieth century. • Main Street Program inspires restoration and improvement of downtown buildings. • California Industrial Products purchases fifty-one acres on Steam Plant Road as site for eighty thousand square foot manufacturing plant; will produce fastener supplies for the automotive industry. • Village Green begins construction of 144 apartment units in first phase of its planned residential-commercial complex on Nashville Pike. • Foxland Hall developers make little progress but deny rumors that their project is for sale. • Byron Charlton and family purchase and assume management of Byron's Bar-B-Q from Beatrice Companies, Inc. • Natural gas system adds six miles of distribution lines. • Built in 1814, Boyers Building on East Main Street is destroyed by fire. • Gallatin Senior High School women's cross-country team wins state championship. • DORCO and ESP are purchased by Ohio manufacturer.

1987 Greater Gallatin, Inc., promotes new downtown street lights. • City scrambles for traffic relief; will consider Airport Road and Maple Street extensions. • Jamison Bedding moves its Nashville manufacturing operations to the former Shaffer Electric Company building. • Servpro Industries moves its home office from California to 575 Airport Road. • Five large residential subdivisions located in and/or adjacent to the city receive planning commission approval. • The Eaton Corporation announces it will close its plant here next year. • Gallatin Senior High School women's basketball team wins state championship.

1988 City Council votes "No" to Sunday beer sales. • LECO Corporation, a Michigan-based firm with a plant in Hendersonville, announces intent to

Gallatin Post Office.

By Allen Haynes

A Time Line History Celebrating the Bicentennial of Gallatin, Tennessee

build a local facility on North Belvedere. • A British firm, Parker-Bath Ltd., locates a small plant here to manufacture therapeutic bathing systems for the elderly. • The YMCA comes to town at 270 East Main Street. • Forty additional public housing units are authorized. • Newly-arrived Trainer Metal Forming, Inc., on Hancock Street will shape metal parts for local GF Furniture. • Despite efforts by the city to locate the new Sumner Administration Building in the downtown area, the County Commission votes to build it on North Belvedere. • County signs contract to build thirty-eight hundred square foot floor space for the Sheriff's Department on West Smith Street. • Rich Products Corporation, a national food processor and distributor, purchases Byron's Bar-B-Q. • Interstate Homes, Inc., a producer of manufactured housing, begins construction of 105,000 square foot plant on Airport Road with factory and equipment representing an investment of $5,720,000. • Mayor appoints Citizens' Blue Ribbon Committee to consider charter revisions, especially to elect aldermen from separate districts and to make the office of mayor a full-time executive position by whatever title. • Halewood Homeowners Association sues planning commission for accepting rights-of-way for Duncan and Joslin Street connectors to the Highway 109 bypass. • City Council hears first proposal for Civic Center, a building for public use and recreational activities.

Clearing the snow, 1985.

Courtesy of Gallatin Department of Electricity

1989 For the first time, women control the City Council holding four of the seven seats. • State DOT begins to clear land for first leg of Highway 109 bypass. • Gallatin Senior High School football team wins AAA state championship in Clinic Bowl. • City issues bonds in amount of $2.8 million for new street construction. • Planning commission seeks to restrict most of Nashville Pike corridor to residential use. • City Council turns down recommendations of blue ribbon Charter Review Committee that included hiring a full-time city

101

Gallatin 200

City Utilities warehouse.

Sumner County Administration Building.

A Time Line History Celebrating the Bicentennial of Gallatin, Tennessee

Rich Products Manufacturing Corporation.

By Allen Haynes

Fleetwood Homes of Tennessee, Inc.

By Allen Haynes

Gallatin 200

Gallatin Waterworks.
By Allen Haynes

Garrott Brothers dock facility.
By Allen Haynes

administrator or manager, eliminating the elective office of recorder by transferring its functions to the Finance Department, hiring a part-time judge for the city court, and electing four council persons at large and three from newly created councilmanic districts. • Bendix-Jidosha Kiki Corporation reveals plans to build new $8 million automotive components plant near the airport; will employ about 120 persons. City purchases site for proposed Civic Center just north of what is to become Albert Gallatin Boulevard. • Local investors organize First Independent Bank.

1990 State begins construction on first leg of Highway 109 Bypass on west side. • Airport Road extension from Coles Ferry Road to Highway 109 South is open for traffic. • Design work is finished for Albert Gallatin Boulevard to connect Dobbins Pike at Highway 109 to U.S. Highway 31-E (Scottsville Pike). • The Gary Company, an independent shirt manufacturer that provided steady employment here for thirty-five years, ceases operations, a casualty to offshore competition. • City Council endorses feasibility study for proposed Civic Center. • City population reaches 18,794.

1991 Cold war ends. Persian Gulf War begins and ends in the same year. • Randy's Record Shop closes after forty-five years in business. • Sumner County Resource Authority begins operating $2.6 million recycling facility. • After acquiring additional land on the south side of Maple Street, Cresent Manufacturing Company purchases the

104

A Time Line History Celebrating the Bicentennial of Gallatin, Tennessee

By Allen Haynes

Sumner Regional Medical Center.

By Allen Haynes

Library Building at Volunteer State Community College.

GALLATIN 200

Medical Plaza at Sumner Regional Medical Center.

By Walter T. Durham

eight-acre Gary Company property adjoining their original site on the north side of Maple. The company adopts five-year plan to build a lumber storage area and a sixty thousand square foot finishing building. • City Council votes bonds to acquire and develop Industrial Park on Airport Road. • Gallatin Senior High School football team is runner-up to AAA state championship losing title game in Clinic Bowl.

1992 Voters elect William Jefferson Clinton president of the United States and Albert Gore Jr. vice president. Gore was well-known here where he had successfully campaigned for seats in the United States House and Senate. • Linatex Corporation of America, a mining equipment manufacturer, moves from Connecticut to one hundred thousand square foot building on Airport Road. • Fleetwood Homes sets up manufactured housing plant in existing building on Airport Road. • Rappahannock Wire Co. announces expansion of current

Gallatin Utilities Office: Gas, Water, Sewer services.

By Allen Haynes

A Time Line History Celebrating the Bicentennial of Gallatin, Tennessee

facilities on Steam Plant Road. • City says Eritech, a North Carolina manufacturer of electrical components for the building trade, will build 150,000 square foot plant in new Industrial Park. • With popular election no longer required, the County School Board selects first superintendent of schools as authorized by new state Education Improvement Act of 1992. • Gallatin Senior High School is state AAA football champion by defeating Clinton High 21–13; ends season without losing a game.

1993 Using two-thirds private gifts and one-third city funds, the city purchased historic Rose Mont. Located one mile south of the Public Square on State Highway 109, it is the first historic site owned by the city. • Second leg of Highway

Loading Dock at GAP. By Allen Haynes

Offices at GAP. By Allen Haynes

GALLATIN 200

Bosch Breaking Systems (formerly Allied Signal). By James W. Thomas

109 Bypass is open for traffic. • Numerous local friends of Albert Gore Jr. attend Clinton-Gore inauguration in Washington. • City acquires thirty-five acres adjoining Municipal Park as site for Civic Center and awards construction contract. • Albert Gallatin Boulevard is open for traffic. • United Chambers of Sumner County hire first tourism director for county. • Continuing archaeological exploration at the site of Isaac Bledsoe's 1790s Fort tantalizes historians of the early settlement period. • Two Gallatin Senior High schoolteachers win Presidential Award for Excellence in Science and Mathematics. • Gallatin earns sixth consecutive Three Star Certification under state Three Star Community Economic Preparedness Program. • City leases from U.S. Corps of Engineers 147-acre lakefront tract for use as

Sumner County Museum exhibit at county fair. By Allen Haynes

A Time Line History Celebrating the Bicentennial of Gallatin, Tennessee

public park at end of Lock Four Road and thirty-four acres on Lower Station Camp Creek Road for use as soccer fields.

1994 Public hearings begin on possible routes for northern loop of Interstate 840. • Civic Center opens. • Wal-Mart announces plans for super store on Nashville Pike; opposition begins fight that ultimately ends in extended litigation. • Trying to improve the city's ability to recruit industry, the council sets up the Industrial Development Board to replace the Economic and Community Development Committee. • Crime in the city increases in almost all categories; police believe it is due to increased illegal traffic in cocaine and crack cocaine. • County builds new Rucker-Stewart Middle School on Hancock Street. • Locally owned AM radio station WMRO succeeds WAMG. • Sumner Regional Medical Center is now operated by Sumner Regional Health Systems, a nonprofit organization that leases the hospital building from Sumner County for one dollar per year. New arrangement will free hospital operations from narrow restrictions in original charter. • Volunteer State Community College opens newly constructed $5.5 million library. Spring semester enrollment reaches total of 5,273 students. • Local economy strong; unemployment is at record lows.

1995 Sumner Regional Medical Center breaks ground for four-story medical office plaza adjoining hospital. It will house first cancer treatment center in the county. • Local crime rates are

Hoeganaes Corporation.   By Allen Haynes

Triple Creek Park.   By Allen Haynes

109

GALLATIN 200

Veterans Memorial on grounds of County Administration Building.

By Allen Haynes

generally lower than in 1994. • One thousand eight hundred eighty-five residential real estate closings set county record. • Greater Gallatin, Inc., plans to renovate Roth's Jewelry Store and restore the Palace Theater next door. • City Council approves creation of Woodson Terrace Historic District. • TVA may bring coal to Gallatin Steam Plant by barge instead of by rail. • GAP announces plans to locate Southeastern U.S. distribution facility here; will build three buildings containing a total of 1.8 million square feet on a 132-acre site behind Volunteer State Community College. Peek employment is expected to reach fifteen hundred. State and local tax dollar incentives to GAP total approximately $1 million that includes construction of roadway link from Vietnam Veterans Boulevard to Highway 109 Bypass. • Congressional proposal to sell Corps of Engineers dams and lakes on the Cumberland River is greeted by strong local opposition. • Feasibility study shows Nashville to Gallatin corridor one of two most likely routes for commuter rail service. • City sells fifteen-acre tract of Industrial Park to Shepherd Products, Inc., a parts supplier to Globe Furniture Co. • Marcar Transportation of Lebanon, Tennessee, will locate terminal in Industrial Park. • City plans to widen Green Wave Drive past Rucker-Stewart Middle School.

1996 Sumner Regional Medical Systems opens new offices in three nearby counties in home health services expansion. • GAPCO employees reject representation by United Auto Workers Union 135–62. • First house built under auspices of Habitat for Humanity of Sumner County is completed. • The German industrial power, the Robert Bosch Group, purchases Allied Signal plant on Belvedere and Allied Signal Jidosha-Kiki on Airport Road. • Victorious in litigation against local opponents of their plans, Wal-Mart begins construction of superstore. • The original Civil War map of the Gallatin area drawn by Union Army Major Willett is on display at the Sumner County Museum. • Infact Corporation says it will construct a new manufacturing and warehouse facility in the Industrial Park. Its products are used by the water utility industry. • City Council votes funds to start computer networking of city offices. • A retired Air Force F-4

110

A Time Line History Celebrating the Bicentennial of Gallatin, Tennessee

By Allen Haynes

Veterans Wall of Honor on grounds of County Administration Building.

Phantom jet arrives at Gallatin Airport for installation in a memorial to Tennessee veterans of military service. • Local postmaster presents Tennessee Bicentennial Stamp with cancellation featuring Trousdale Place. • A city held referendum approves liquor by the drink 3,662 to 2,924.

1997 Coal trains become things of the past and no longer block local street crossings as TVA shifts coal delivery from rail to river barges. • Sumner Foundation opens hospitality house for out-of-town families with members requiring hospitalization. • Former employees of Genesco, corporate successor to the Jarman Shoe Company and later General Shoe Company, stage reunion at old Factory Lane plant site. • Per capita income countywide reaches $22,823, just under the national level but showing the fastest growth rate in the United States. • The Department of Transportation promises to make a four-lane road of State Highway 109 between Gallatin and Portland. • Growth of local economy is outstripping the state and national averages. • Gallatin has sixty-five manufacturing plants employing 5,515 persons. • Hoeganaes, with eighth furnace just installed, reveals plans for $33.6 million expansion including two additional furnaces and other improvements; expansion will increase production from current level of 220,000 tons of ferrous metal powders to 260,000 tons. • Western Reserve Plastics discontinues production here and discharges 120 workers but keeps office and distribution center with 50 employees. • City purchases 180 acres for new Triple Creek Park.

1998 Gallatin and the White House Utility District negotiate deal on sewer service for Douglas Bend, Cage's Bend, and Station Camp Creek areas that invites further residential development. • As GAP finishes third building on its 132-acre campus, the company becomes the largest employer in the county with one thousand persons on payroll. • GF Office Furniture begins construction of one hundred thousand square foot distribution center on Airport Road. • Gallatin and Hendersonville agree to a planned growth scheme that establishes adjoining borders. • City adopts new land use plan and passes supporting ordinances. • Several new stores, restaurants, and motels boost retail trade. • The state withholds Three Star rating, perceiving

GALLATIN 200

1999
ECONOMIC DEVELOPMENT AGENCY
(EDA)

With the formation of the Economic Development Agency by the Gallatin City Council in 1999 and the hiring of a full-time recruiter and office staff, Gallatin's economic and industrial development efforts changed from "reactive" to "proactive." The focus now is on the full scope of economic development that includes retail and office as well as industrial recruitment.

Through the years, as a result of the dedicated work of several volunteer recruiters and the Industrial Development Board, Gallatin's industrial base developed significantly. However, the focus was primarily on industrial recruitment.

The EDA office is now a one-stop source for business location information and sends promotional materials to potential prospects through a growing marketing program.

less aggressive business recruiting activity by the community. • Construction of Vena Stuart Elementary School is underway at 780 Hart Street. • Shafer Middle School building is completed at 240 Albert Gallatin Avenue. • Volunteer State Community College baseball team ends season ranked number one nationwide among junior colleges. • Manufacturing jobs decline 5.7 percent over prior year.

1999 City establishes Economic Development Agency, appropriates funds for its budget, and hires director. • Gallatin regains state Three Star status. • Newest city park, Triple Creek, wins award of excellence from the Greater Nashville Regional Council. • City launches further development of soccer complex on the west side. • Tornado rips through the Greenwood Apartment complex on Green Wave Drive and also extensively damages the post office on Maple Street. • The women's basketball team of Gallatin Senior High School wins AAA state

championship. • Mushrooming construction is expected on a total of 876 lots adjacent to Brown's Lane approved by planning commission. • A fast-growing national chain contractor supply company purchases Durham Building Supply. • Public applauds Chamber of Commerce July 4 fireworks show; expects it to be an annual event. • Locating bike paths and walking trails may become a city government function. • Gallatin Housing Authority is remodeling and upgrading its older units. • GAP official delivers check for $175,000 to city as a contribution for reworking and widening a portion of Harris Lane. • Volunteer State Community College acquires next door site formerly owned by Rebound, Inc. It includes five buildings on 9.8 acres. • The American Legion Post 17 baseball team wins the Legion's Southeastern Regional Championship but loses in semifinal game of the Legion World Series. • Gallatin joins eight other cities in the county to project their boundary lines twenty years out and to publish a map of the projections.

2000 Albert Gore Jr. leads George W. Bush by more than five hundred thousand popular votes nationwide, but after the U.S. Supreme Court stops the recount in Florida, Bush wins the presidency in the Electoral College. • Work begins on widening Harris Lane and West Eastland and extension of Sumner Hall Drive to Belvedere. • An announcement is made for a new building to house the Sumner County Health Department. It will be called the Dodson Health Department Building and is to be located on Dobbins Pike about two hundred yards north of Albert Gallatin Boulevard. • County ponders possible relocation of jail. • Plans for new school buildings include a new Union Elementary School in Gallatin and a new high school on Station Camp Creek Road between Hendersonville and Gallatin. Initially, the high school will take students from Hendersonville, Beech, and Gallatin schools. • A Gallatin Senior High School teacher is the third from school to

112

A Time Line History Celebrating the Bicentennial of Gallatin, Tennessee

Cragfont garden.

win a Presidential Award for Excellence in Science and Mathematics. • State Department of Transportation begins right-of-way acquisition for extension of Vietnam Veterans Boulevard from Avondale to Gallatin. • City population is 23,230. • TVA installs four more natural gas or oil-fired combustion turbines at Gallatin Steam Plant.

2001 Mayor Don Wright appoints a citizens committee to plan a proper observance of the city's two hundred birthday in 2002. • Cresent Manufacturing Company has extended its Maple Street plant facility to thirty-nine acres including five hundred

Cragfont, rear addition.

113

Gallatin 200

By Allen Haynes

American Veterans Memorial and F-4 Fighter Monument at airport.

thousand square feet under roof. • Ellen Wemyss, the gracious mistress of Fairvue Plantation and lifelong historical preservationist, dies at the age of 106 years. • Residential development of Fairvue proceeds; it is called "The Last Plantation." • Air Force F-4 Fighter Monument is dedicated at Gallatin Airport by American Legion John T. Alexander Post 17 as a memorial to all United States veterans of military service. • St. John Vianney announces plans to build and operate an elementary school on North Water Street near the church. • County takes options on West Smith and West Bledsoe Street properties adjoining and/or near the Sumner County Jail for prospective construction of extensive additions to present facility. • On September 11, Gallatin is shocked by tragic news that terrorist hijackers had intentionally crashed commercial airliners into the twin towers of the World Trade Center in New York and into the Pentagon near Washington. Most agree that it is an attack on America but by whom? Local churches have special prayer services for victims; Red Cross appeals for blood and receives quick response.

2000
Gore Wins Gallatin Vote

During the national campaign, GOP vice presidential candidate Dick Cheney spoke to a partisan audience at a Gallatin campaign rally. On the same day former Governor Ned McWherter countered at a mass meeting for Democratic presidential candidate Albert Gore Jr. On Election Day in the boxes traditionally regarded as Gallatin precincts, voters cast 3,073 votes for Gore and 2,562 for George W. Bush.

Epilogue

Now clearly across the threshold into a new millennium, Gallatin faces the prospect of accelerated change with an equanimity developed over its two-hundred-year journey from frontier town to sophisticated small city.

Immediately ahead is the near certainty that the extensive development of residential properties will further change a familiar rural landscape while making major contributions to the local economy for the next ten to twenty years. The market for housing will be supported not only by other economic development within the city but by the growth of Nashville and the need for homes for persons who work there. It will be assisted additionally by improved individual earnings that will enable would-be buyers to translate dreams of home ownership into twenty-first century reality.

Undoubtedly, changes noted recently in the manufacturing sector will continue with the resultant exit of some factories and the arrival of others. As in the past, local investors will have opportunities to establish and operate production facilities and some will surely do so. Local firms of many kinds will be affected by the surging service industry, but exactly how and when is a matter yet to be determined. The presence of the massive GAP distribution center is a reminder that Gallatin is well located geographically for distributing goods and services. Midway between the Gulf of Mexico and the Great Lakes, it is appealingly close to the population center of the United States.

The economic development program now in place, underwritten and overseen by the city, has serious potential for nurturing local commerce and increasing the tax base. A declining farm population and the diminishing supply of farmland combine to make it very unlikely that the city will ever reclaim its earlier role as a service center for producers of agricultural products.

As the General Assembly and governor wrestle with the costs of higher education, the pressure to consolidate certain state colleges and universities will increase, leaving the future of some of the institutions in grave doubt. Thirty-one years of successful operation here since its founding in 1971 does much to assure that "Vol State" will remain one of the stellar community colleges in the country. Careers enhanced by study at the college will contribute increasingly to the skill of our work force and to the quality of life in the region.

We can expect the local and national passion for improved education in elementary and secondary schools to result in further examination of the learning process and the results it produces. Debates about adequate funding for schools, test results, and the accountability of administrators and teachers will go on beyond tomorrow as we try to reconcile the importance we attach to education with the amount of money we are willing to invest in it. Fortunately, the Sumner County Board of Education, which serves Gallatin, has developed a school system that seems strong enough to accommodate change with a minimum of stress. The presence of the private schools—Sumner Academy (independent), College Heights Christian Academy (Baptist), and St. John Vianney (Catholic)—can enrich the mix and enliven the process.

GALLATIN 200

Perhaps the most difficult experiences ahead lie in the area of human relationships. The future of this community will depend in no small part on how well we live together as neighbors. The Judeo-Christian tradition, the faith of preference for a large majority of Gallatin people, invokes spiritual standards in human relations that can be helpful to its adherents and others, as well. In addition to the ministry of local churches in support of this tradition, many civic and fraternal organizations exist for the primary purpose of serving others, the ultimate neighborliness. Can this be a local confluence of the spiritual and the pragmatic from which brotherhood will flow?

For the rest of this century the challenges are plentiful. Three especially call for our attention: A changing economy; a closer involvement with educating our young; and a need to foster neighborliness and a sense of community among all of our people.

This is a new frontier, but historically we are a frontier people. We can meet the challenges.

Appendix A

THESE MEN AND WOMEN DELIVER FOR GALLATIN

Important in their individual persons as citizens, the employees of the city of Gallatin are important to the rest of the citizenry as providers of a wide range of services that vary from fire and police protection to leisure services. Most persons employed by the city work in the offices of the mayor, the recorder, six departments, four separate divisions, an agency, four commissions, and the independent but closely related Department of Electricity.

The department heads are: Walter Tangel, chief of police; Joe M. Womack, fire chief; David F. Brown, director of leisure services; David A. Gregory, superintendent of public utilities; Rebecca Hayes, director of finance; and Ronnie Stiles, superintendent of public works. In addition to the department heads, the following lead important city divisions: Ron Coleman, city engineer; Elaine Nichols, interim building official; Jim Svoboda, city planner; and David Crawford, personnel director. The city attorney is Joe H. Thompson.

Tommy G. Burns is the executive director of the Economic Development Agency. Members of the EDA Board are Tim Galvin, David Schreiner, and L. A. Green.

A Municipal-Regional Planning Commission deals with planning issues and zoning. The chair is James Robert Ramsey. Commission members are Dick Dempsey, vice chair; Thomas Richey, secretary; Albert A. Bennett, Rosemary Bates, Ed Mayberry, and Mayor Don Wright. Jimmy Moore presides over the Board of Municipal Zoning Appeals, and David Choby presides over the Regional Board of Zoning Appeals. Rosemary Bates is chair of the Historic Zoning Commission.

Mickey Avaritt is the head professional and Richard D. Tayes is the golf course superintendent at Long Hollow Golf Course. The municipally owned and operated course is governed by a Golf Course Commission whose members are Frank Brinkley, Richard Stephenson, Daryl Holt, P. M. "Pete" Green, and Jim Ford.

Another commission and board have important functions. Skip Sparkman is chair of the Cable Commission that is charged with making recommendations to the council on matters having to do with the cable franchise. The Beer Board acts on applications made through the recorder's office. The board chair is David Brown Parrish.

Created by the city, the Department of Electricity operates independently with a three-member board appointed by the mayor with the concurrence of the council. John R. Phillips Sr. is chairman with board members Dr. J. Deotha Malone and Ed Mayberry. Bill Draper is manager of the department.

Providing a significant assortment of low income housing, the Gallatin Housing Authority is an independent body. Kurt Tschaepe is executive director. Board members of the authority are appointed by the mayor.

Other employees of the city, excluding the mayor and recorder, are listed here alphabetically by position.

Administrative secretary—Patricia S. McWhirter, Patty A. Rose-DeWitt, Jacqueline Hoyle.
Animal control officer—Timothy P. Anschuetz.
Aquatics supervisor—Charles C. Burgett.
Assistant director of public utilities—Rollow M. Carpenter.
Assistant fire chief—William L. Crook.

GALLATIN 200

Captain of operations—Dennis A. Thrasher.

Cashier—Kathi A. Kirby, Heather Lo.

Cemetery clerk/groundskeeper—Tony C. Fuqua.

Chief water plant operator—Bennie J. Baggett.

Chief inspector—Joseph M. Crass.

Chief wastewater plant operator—Steve R. Gibson.

Civic center assistant—Robert E. Riley III, Steven C. Brown, Christie Simpson.

Clubhouse assistant—J. Dick McClure.

Clubhouse manager—Michael L. Avaritt.

Codes inspector I—Arthur W. Brese.

Crew leader—Troy W. Martin, James W. Wheeler, Clyde Sexton, Mike E. McDonald.

Crew supervisor—Bobby F. Criner, Jeffrey L. Starnes.

Custodian I—G. Eugene Watson.

Custodian II—Rose Russell.

Customer service clerk I—Kathy Stewart, Tana Dorris, Diesha Turner, Debbie Graves, Carrie Graves.

Customer service clerk II—Cindy L. Brazel, Amy D. Summers, Betty S. Crecelius.

Customer service supervisor—Sheila G. Sorrells, Dora L. Tippit.

Engineering technician—Gary L. Jones.

Equipment maintenance superintendent—James L. Loper Jr.

Equipment mechanic—Steve L. Satterfield, James S. Summers, William Mark Sullivan.

Equipment technician—Brian Keith, Johnny Ray Brown.

Executive secretary—Vickie Willoughby, Deborah Wilson, Day Horner, Janis S. Myers, Jeanette Oakley, Diane R. Allers.

Facility maintenance supervisor—Lyndon S. Satterfield.

Finance/account clerk—Celila F. Burgett, Dianna White.

Fire captain—Homer Barr, Ferrell L. Fuqua, Kenneth L. Weidner.

Fire dispatcher—James E. Butler, William Haynes, James D. Civils.

Fire lieutenant—Robert E. Richie Jr., John R. Parker Jr., Robert L. Smith.

Fire marshall—J. Stan Gwaltney.

Fire shift captain—Larry J. Fuqua, Richard J. Roberts, Walter T. Dale Jr.

Firefighter—Mark A. Sullivan, David S. Woodard, Benjamin A. Harris, Mark E. Hall, Darrick D. York, Cless E. Summers, Brian D. Denning, Ernest J. DiPhillipo, Teddy D. Baird, Rodney W. Pryor, Brandon Howell, Grover John Sharp.

Firefighter/engineer—Larry Meadors, Ralph R. Collier, Webb A. Canter, Willie R. DeBow, Bobby J. Coward, Steven P. Brewington, James A. Workings, Henry W. Shaw, Mark Jenkins, Johnny M. Johnson, Robert M. Parrish, Jeffrey T. Broadrick.

Gas line welder—Christopher Estes.

Gas service technician—Robert S. Whited, James E. Lee, Denver D. Ausbrooks.

Gas service worker—Stephen L. Vantrease, Billy W. Downs, George L. Toenyes.

General worker/operator—Jimmy D. McCall, William Breedlove, Michael F. Parker, Charles Kevin Templeton, William Horace Lauper.

General supervisor—Randall L. James, Roger Thurber, Curtis P. Brummett, Roger L. Clemons, Clarence F. Southall.

General worker—James E. Young, Mitchell Currey, Garey Taylor, Seth Adam Terrell, Jason Williams.

Groundskeeper—Tommy Strother, Johnny D. Morris, Arthur Hatt, Michael Watkins, Anthony Thompson, Jessie Cole.

Inmate crew leader—James R. McWhirter.

Interim city engineer—Ronald M. Coleman.

Interim director of finance—Eve I. Kim.

Inventory/records clerk—Samuel P. Reynolds.

Lead deputy clerk—Marcella Weese.

Leisure services assistant/maintenance—Wade A. Bruce.

Major—Caldwell Jenkins.

Mayor's assistant—Tammy J. DeMeio

Meter reader—Michael B. Ridings, Rayburn M. Smith, J. Doug Parks, Richard R. Berger.

Motor equipment operator III—Steven F. Scherrer, Kevin Woodall, Danny Lyles, Frank A. Sircy, Thomas A. Petty, Donald R. Carter.

Parks and recreation assistant—Elaine Hudson.

Permit specialist—Becky L. Pardue.

Personnel specialist—Becky T. McWhorter.

Planner I—Shannon Bell-Logan.

Planner II—Sharon G. Burton.

A Time Line History Celebrating the Bicentennial of Gallatin, Tennessee

Police aide/custodian—James S. Daniels.

Police communications supervisor—Amanda Brown

Police dispatcher—Marsha Ayers, Mary E. Jaques, Faye B. Haynes, Vickie Campbell, Kimberly D. McCullough, Neil Toll.

Police lieutenant—Susan F. Morrow, Robert J. Helson, Ronald L. Parker, Earl W. Hall.

Police officer—Michael K. Gilbert, Janell M. Wilson, Phillip Woodard, Walter E. Gray II, Jody L. Starks, John Michael Jones, Shay R. McBride, Scott C. Conaway, Gary Lee Chansler Jr., Glenn E. Hesson, A. Jamie Pack, Jason Elliott, Danny K. Deyhle, Reuben J. Dobson, Richard T. Evans, Gerald S. Woodard, David T. Lo, Mark E. Hill, Charlie E. Harris, Gail E. Humes, Donald W. Bandy, Danny Strope, Jeff D. Petty, Harold G. Perry, John P. Smith, Willis L. Ballard, Julie J. Patterson, Ronald Black, Rickey Allen Troup, William Vahldiek Jr., William J. McCrory, Bennett C. Adams, Larry J. Burke Jr., Douglas Leon Harris, Bradley A. Nave, Gregory N. Arias, Justin Croniser.

Police records/communication supervisor—Candace R. Brown

Police records clerk—Mary M. Nighbert, Madalena E. Hutcheson.

Police sergeant—Kate J. Novitsky, William J. Sorrels, Betty L. Smith, Gregory A. Bunch.

Public service officer—Frances L. Jackson, Jean Donoho, Carney Troutt.

Pump station technician—Russell H. Wix.

Quality control inspector—Richard L. Burton.

Recreation programs supervisor—A. Page Jackson.

Sanitation crew leader—Benny L. Tillman, James H. Dalton, Rayburn L. Carter Jr., Charles A. Workings.

Sanitation equipment operator II—Jackie Gregory, Bobby Stewart, Michael Robertson, John Robert Bush, Bobby E. Chestnutt.

Sanitation worker—Steven R. Gilbert, T. Brad Johnson, Richard E. Smith, James A. Burton.

Secretary—Lori W. Ragland.

Sign and marking technician—Charles L. Whitney.

Senior fire inspector—Mark F. Schultz.

Staff services supervisor—Candi K. Bullock.

Switchboard/permit clerk—Becky V. Brown.

Switchboard—Stephanie Starnes.

Traffic control officer—Mary E. Dodd, Marie F. Smith.

TV inspection/sealing technician—Charles E. Swindle.

Utility billing clerk—April L. Sartain.

Utility dispatcher—Billy R. Beasley.

Utility maintenance supervisor—James T. Moody.

Utility plant assistant—William E. Ellis, James H. Rice.

Utility plant attendant—Jesse J. Beasley, Christopher Conner, Frank E. Muse.

Utility plant technician—Viren F. Patel, David L. McConnell.

Utility service technician—David L. Shackelford, Billy Joe Burns, Jerry L. Conyer, Frankie L. Meador, Ricky N. Fulkerson.

Utility service worker—B. Scott Carr, Daniel J. Gammon, Kevin Terry, L. E. Freeman, James H. Lee, James D. Huffman II.

Utility operation support—David T. Kellogg.

Wastewater plant operator—Bobby R. Tucker.

Water plant operator—Jerry R. Alexander.

The employees of the Department of Electricity in addition to the manager are:

Office manager—Rebecca Rippy.

Engineer—Michael Taylor.

Line foreman—Ronald Johnson.

Meter technician—Richard Pryor.

Accountant—George Anderson.

Apprentice lineman—Mark Denning.

Cashier/customer service—Sandra Carey, Suzanne Clark, Donna Jenkins.

Clerk—Susan Gregory, Sharon Hebb, Melody Lauderdale, Faye Saunders.

Custodian—Suzanne Burgett.

Executive secretary—Rita Simpson.

Field engineer—Jimmie Gillihan.

Groundman—David Barnes, Richard Key, Joseph Walker.

Lineman—Joe Bailey, Johnny Perry, James Smith, Steve Swanson.

Meter reader—Troy Dawes, Robert Hall.

Meter service—Gordon Carman.

Stores clerk—Stanley Weese.

Working line foreman—Stanley Duffer.

Part-time clerk—Gayla Templeton, Sharon Williams.

Appendix B

CONGRATULATORY LETTERS

Gallatin's two-hundredth birthday is a time of self-congratulation for its citizens. For others, it is a time to express congratulations to the people of the county seat of the fifth oldest county in Tennessee. And there seems to be no hesitation on the part of either.

Self-congratulations are self-evident. The people of Gallatin are taking nearly an entire year to celebrate the occasion and are doing it in a variety of ways. Some appear very smug about the whole affair, and others are excited about the yesterday-today-tomorrow comparisons that are implicit in any such celebration.

The response to the bicentennial from afar has been positive and complimentary. Although there is no way to reproduce the hundreds of verbal greetings that have been sent this way, it is appropriate to share selected congratulatory letters from ranking public officials of national, state, and county governments. The sentiments expressed confirm local conviction that this is a significant birthday in the life of Gallatin. They recognize also that this American city is proud of its past, is grateful for the quality of life it now enjoys, and is confident of a promising future.

SENATOR BILL FRIST
WASHINGTON, D.C.

July, 2002

The Honorable Don Wright
Mayor
City of Gallatin
132 West Main Street
Gallatin, TN 37066

Dear Don:

    Karyn and I send our warmest greetings and sincere congratulations on the 200th birthday celebration of the City of Gallatin. What a tremendous milestone in the history of your community.

    Two hundred years have transformed the face of Gallatin. We now enjoy a level of prosperity unimaginable in 1802, but the keys to a good life are the same. When Tennesseans work hard and care for each other, they do well and our communities prosper. Let us pledge to lay such a strong foundation for the next century that when citizens of Gallatin gather to celebrate in 2102, they will speak of our age with gratitude and respect.

    My very best wishes to each of you for a wonderful celebration.

Warm regards,

Bill Frist
United States Senator

FRED THOMPSON
TENNESSEE

COMMITTEES:

GOVERNMENTAL AFFAIRS

FINANCE

INTELLIGENCE

United States Senate

WASHINGTON, DC 20510–4204
http://thompson.senate.gov

June 15, 2001

Mayor Don Wright
City of Gallatin
132 W. Main St.
Gallatin, Tennessee 37066

Dear Mayor Wright:

I would like to congratulate the City of Gallatin on its 200th
Birthday. The residents of Gallatin should be filled with pride
in knowing they live in a town immersed in so much history and
rich heritage.

It is nice to see a people-oriented community be so well
preserved. I wish you many more successful centuries.

Again, congratulations for reaching such a milestone.

Sincerely,

Fred Thompson
United States Senator

FT:kao

BART GORDON 6TH DISTRICT, TENNESSEE COMMITTEES: ENERGY AND COMMERCE SCIENCE **RANKING MEMBER** SUBCOMMITTEE: SPACE AND AERONAUTICS	 **Congress of the United States** **House of Representatives**	2368 RAYBURN BUILDING WASHINGTON, DC 20515-4206 (202) 225-4231 FAX: (202) 225-6887 106 SOUTH MAPLE STREET P.O. BOX 1986 MURFREESBORO, TN 37133 (615) 896-1986 FAX: (615) 896-8218 15 SOUTH JEFFERSON STREET P.O. BOX 1140 COOKEVILLE, TN 38501 (931) 528-5907

August 14, 2001

Walter T. Durham, President
Gallatin Bicentennial Celebration Committee Inc.
338-B Sumner Hall Drive
Gallatin, TN 37066-3129

Dear Friends,

    I congratulate the city of Gallatin on its 200th birthday. Reaching such a grand milestone deserves an all-out celebration.

    Gallatin's 23,230 residents are truly blessed to live in such a progressive community. Carved out of the Middle Tennessee wilderness in 1802, the county seat of Sumner County was named for Albert Gallatin. He was secretary of the Treasury Department for both Presidents Thomas Jefferson and James Madison. Today the town has a proud legacy steeped in honor and tradition.

    From its modest pioneer beginnings, Gallatin has prospered into a modern community full of desirable attributes. Its leaders, both past and present, have shown much forethought in creating a quality of life second to none.

    I am proud to serve a city that has such a rich heritage. Once again, I congratulate Gallatin and its leaders for their vision in building a city of enviable diversity, friendship and tradition.

                                                  Sincerely,

                                                 BART GORDON
                                                 Member of Congress

STATE OF TENNESSEE

DON SUNDQUIST
GOVERNOR

January 1, 2002

Dear Friends:

As Governor, it is a privilege to offer warm wishes and congratulations to you on the occasion of the City of Gallatin's 200th Anniversary. I know that this is an exciting time for the proud citizens of Gallatin.

As you celebrate your Bicentennial, I hope you will take the opportunity to reflect on the long history and rich heritage of Gallatin. This city has been home to many remarkable Tennesseans and continues to be a fine example of the very best of the Volunteer State.

Again, congratulations on Gallatin's 200th Anniversary. Martha and I extend our every good wish for continued success and progress.

Warm regards,

Don Sundquist

DS/mgf

State Capitol, Nashville, Tennessee 37243-0001
Telephone No. (615) 741-2001

Metropolitan Government of Nashville and Davidson County

Bill Purcell Mayor

August 10, 2001

Greetings:

Congratulations to Gallatin, Tennessee as you recognize the 200th Anniversary of your birth. I am proud to join in the celebration of this illustrious and significant occasion.

Gallatin has proven over the years to be one of Nashville's most industrious and remarkable neighbors. Old Hickory Lake has been a favorite destination for many Nashville citizens, as well as Volunteer State Community College. Gallatin played an integral role in the development of Middle Tennessee's history.

I wish you continued success in all your future endeavors, as we always remain "good neighbors".

Again, congratulations!

Sincerely,

Bill Purcell
Mayor

Office of the Mayor
Metropolitan Courthouse
Nashville, Tennessee 37201
Phone: 615.862.6000
Fax: 615.862.6040
mayor@metro.nashville.org

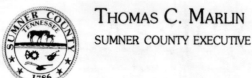

THOMAS C. MARLIN

SUMNER COUNTY EXECUTIVE

"A Pleasure to Serve You"

December 31, 2001

The Honorable Don Wright
Mayor, City of Gallatin
132 West Main Street
Gallatin, Tennessee 37066

Dear Mayor Wright:

It is with heartfelt best wishes that I congratulate the City of Gallatin, our county seat town, on its 200th anniversary. On the occasion of this bicentennial celebration, we reflect on our past and look forward with great anticipation to our bright future.

Gallatin enjoys a history rich in tradition and friendship. This foundation will continue to direct Gallatin as it grows and prospers in this century.

Again, congratulations on this historic event.

Sincerely,

Thomas C. Marlin
Sumner County Executive

TCM/le

355 NORTH BELVEDERE DRIVE • ROOM 102 • GALLATIN, TENNESSEE 37066-5413 • (615) 452-3604

Selected Bibliography

Books

Adams, Henry. *The Life of Albert Gallatin*. Philadelphia: J. B. Lippincott & Co., 1879.

Albright, Edward. *Early History of Middle Tennessee*. Nashville, Tenn.: Brandon Printing Co., 1909.

Anderson, James Douglas. *The Historic Blue Grass Line*. Nashville, Tenn.: Nashville-Gallatin Interurban Railway, 1913.

_____. *Making the American Thoroughbred, Especially in Tennessee, 1800–1845.* Norwood, Mass.: The Plimpton Press, 1916.

Baskerville, J. T., comp. and rev. *Laws and Ordinances of the Corporation of Gallatin.* Nashville, Tenn.: City of Gallatin, 1911.

Biographical Directory of the American Congress, 1774–1949. Washington, D.C.: U.S. Government Printing Office, 1950.

Biographical Directory of the Tennessee General Assembly. Vols. I (1796–1861) and 2 (1861–1901). Robert M. McBride and Daniel M. Robison, eds., published by Tennessee Historical Commission and Tennessee State Library and Archives, 1975–1979; Vols. III–VI (1901–1991). Ilene J. Cornwell, ed., published by Tennessee Historical Commission, 1988–1991.

Brandau, Roberta Seawell, ed. *History of Homes and Gardens of Tennessee*. Nashville, Tenn.: Parthenon Press, 1936.

Brinkley, Velma Howell and Mary Huddleston Malone. *Generations. A Pictorial Journey into the Lives of African Americans in Sumner County, Tennessee, 1796–1996*. Nashville, Tenn.: Morgan Publications, 1996.

_____. *African-American Life in Sumner County*. Dover, N. H.: Arcadia Publishing, 1998.

Caldwell, Joshua W. *Sketches of the Bench and Bar of Tennessee*. Knoxville, Tenn.: Ogden and Brothers Co., Printers, 1898.

Carr, John. *Early Times in Middle Tennessee*. Reprint. Nashville, Tenn.: Robert H. Horsley and Associates, 1958.

Cisco, J. Guy. *Historic Sumner County, Tennessee*. Nashville, Tenn.: Folk-Keelin Printing Co., 1909.

Clark, Isaac. *Clark's Miscellany in Prose and Verse*. Nashville, Tenn.: T. G. Bradford, 1812.

Douglas, Byrd. *Steamboatin' on the Cumberland*. Nashville, Tenn.: Tennessee Book Company, 1961.

Duke, Basil W. *A History of Morgan's Cavalry*. Cecil Fletcher Holland, ed. Bloomington: Indiana University Press, 1960.

Durham, Walter T. *A College for This Community*. Gallatin, Tenn.: Sumner County Library Board, 1974.

_____. *Daniel Smith, Frontier Statesman*. Gallatin, Tenn.: Sumner County Library Board, 1976.

_____. *The Great Leap Westward, A History of Sumner County, Tennessee, From Its Beginnings to 1805*. Gallatin, Tenn.: Sumner County

GALLATIN 200

Library Board, 1969. (Reprinted, 1993, Gallatin, Sumner County Archives).

_____. *James Winchester, Tennessee Pioneer.* Gallatin, Tenn.: Sumner County Library Board, 1979.

_____. *Old Sumner, A History of Sumner County, Tennessee, From 1805 to 1861.* Gallatin, Tenn.: Sumner County Library Board, 1972.

_____. *Rebellion Revisited, A History of Sumner County, Tennessee, From 1861 to 1870.* Gallatin, Tenn.: Sumner County Museum Association, 1982. (Reprinted, 1999, Sumner County Archives.)

_____. *Volunteer Forty-Niners: Tennesseans and the California Gold Rush.* Nashville, Tenn.: Vanderbilt University Press, 1997.

_____. *Wynnewood, Bledsoe's Lick, Castalian Springs, Tennessee.* Castalian Springs, Tenn.: Bledsoe's Lick Historical Association, Inc., 1994.

Durham, Walter T. and James W. Thomas. *A Pictorial History of Sumner County, Tennessee, 1796–1986.* Gallatin, Tenn.: Sumner County Historical Society, 1986.

Durham, Walter T., James W. Thomas, and John F. Creasy. *A Celebration of Houses Built Before 1900 in Sumner County, Tennessee.* Gallatin, Tenn.: Sumner County Historical Society, 1995.

Ferguson, Edwin L. *Sumner County, Tennessee in the Civil War.* Tompkinsville, Ky.: Monroe County Press, 1972.

Fitch, John. *Annals of the Army of the Cumberland.* Philadelphia: J. B. Lippincott, & Co., 1864.

Guild, George B. *A Brief Narrative of the Fourth Tennessee Cavalry Regiment, Wheeler's Corps, Army of Tennessee.* Nashville, Tenn.: N.p., 1913.

Guild, Josephus Conn. *Old Times in Tennessee.* Nashville, Tenn.: Tavel, Eastman and Howell, 1878.

Hall, William. *Early History of the Southwest.* Reprint. Nashville, Tenn.: The Parthenon Press, 1968.

History of Tennessee, From the Earliest Time to the Present; Together with an Historical and Biographical Sketch of the Counties of Sumner, Smith, Macon and Trousdale, Besides a Valuable fund of Notes, Original Observations, Reminiscences, Etc., Etc. Nashville, Tenn.: The Goodspeed Publishing Co., 1887.

Lester, Dee Gee and Kenneth Calvin Thomson Jr. *Around Gallatin and Sumner County.* Dover, N. H.: Arcadia Publishing, 1998.

_____. *Around Gallatin and Sumner County.* Vol. II. Charleston, S.C.: Arcadia Publishing, 1998.

Morris, Eastin. *The Tennessee Gazetteer.* Nashville, Tenn.: W. Hassell Hunt & Co., 1834.

Read, Opie. *I Remember.* New York: The Branwell Press, 1930.

Russell, Oscar, comp. and rev. *Laws and Ordinances of the Corporation of Gallatin to Which is Prefixed the Charter and to Which is Affixed Bond Issues, Franchises Granted and a Roster of Officials Since the year 1922.* Gallatin, Tenn.: City of Gallatin, 1929.

Snider, Margaret Cummings, and Joan Hollis Yorgason, comps. *Sumner County, Tennessee, Cemetery Records.* Owensboro, Ky.: McDowell Publications, 1981.

Stephenson, Wendell Holmes. *Isaac Franklin, Slaver Trader and Planter of the Old South; With Plantation Records.* Baton Rouge: Louisiana State University Press, 1938.

Warden, Margaret Lindsley. *The Saga of Fairvue, 1832–1977.* Nashville, Tenn.: N.p., 1977.

West, Carroll Van, ed. *The Tennessee Encyclopedia of History and Culture.* Nashville, Tenn.: Tennessee Historical Society and Rutledge Hill Press, 1998.

Wilson, Shirley. *Sumner County, Tennessee. Index to the Loose Records: 1786 to 1930.* Hendersonville, Tenn.: Richley Enterprises, 1988.

Wilson, Sumner A., comp. and rev. *Laws and Ordinances of the Corporation of Gallatin to which is Prefixed the Original Charter with Subsequent Amendments.* Gallatin, Tenn.: City of Gallatin, 1888.

Articles

Allen, Ward. "Cragfont: Grandeur on the Tennessee Frontier." *Tennessee Historical Quarterly,* Vol. XXIII, No. 2, 1964.

A Time Line History Celebrating the Bicentennial of Gallatin, Tennessee

Durham, Walter T. "Civil War Revolver Spins a Tale." *The Gun Report*, Vol. 43, No. 5 (Oct. 1997).

_____. "How Say You, Senator Fowler?" *Tennessee Historical Quarterly*, Vol. XLII, No. 1, 1983.

_____. "James Winchester." *Franklin County Historical Review*, Vol. XX, No. 1, 1989.

_____. "James Winchester, The Ill-Starred General of Sumner County." *Cumberland* (Quarterly), Vol. 2, No. 1, (Winter, 1978).

_____. "Morgan at Gallatin." *Confederate Veteran*, Vol. XXXIV, No. 5 (Nov.–Dec., 1986).

_____. "Tennessee Countess." *Tennessee Historical Quarterly*, Vol. XXXIX, No. 3, 1980.

_____. "Thomas Sharp Spencer, Man or Legend." *Tennessee Historical Quarterly*, Vol. XXXI, No. 3, 1972.

_____. "Westward With Anthony Bledsoe: The Life of an Overmountain Frontier Leader." *Tennessee Historical Quarterly*, Vol. LIII, No. 1, 1994.

Durham, Walter T., ed. "The Arrest: North to Fort Mackinac." *Tennessee Historical Quarterly*, Vol. LV, No. 4, 1996.

_____, ed. "Looking Every Minute for Them to Come." *Tennessee Historical Quarterly*, Vol. LIX, No. 2, 2000.

_____, ed. "Mexican War Letter of George F. Crocket." *Tennessee Historical Quarterly*, Vol. LIII, No. 2, 1994.

Franklin, John Hope. "James T. Ayers, Civil War Recruiter." *Journal of the Illinois State Historical Society*, Vol. XL (Sept. 1947).

Guild, George B. "Reconstruction Times in Sumner County." *The American Historical Magazine*, Vol. VIII (Oct. 1903).

Trousdale, Julius A. "A History of the Life of General William Trousdale." *Tennessee Historical Magazine*, II, No. 2 (June 1916).

Other Sources

Most of the books listed here contain bibliographies that mention other books and articles relating to Gallatin. In addition, they list newspapers, magazines, and manuscript materials that can be greatly helpful to a serious student of almost any aspect of the history of the city.

The minutes of the City Council of Gallatin of 1822 and from 1831–2002 contain important and at times entertaining accounts of the ruminations and actions of that body. No official papers of the city have survived for the period 1802–1822 nor from 1823–1831. Spared the ravages of fire, war, and time, the records of the county of Sumner are remarkably complete, however. In the loose court records at the Sumner Archives one can find almost anything he or she may be looking for!

Although runs of eighteenth century Gallatin newspapers are sadly incomplete, the preserved copies of that period on microfilm plus a much fuller representation from the twentieth century provide illuminating insights into the life of the city and its people. The Sumner County Archives has microfilm copies of all known surviving issues of Gallatin newspapers.

The Tennessee State Library and Archives, Nashville, holds an incredible range of materials pertaining to Gallatin including Tennessee newspaper files, militia lists, land records, papers from the state archives, and an untold number of manuscripts.

The records of the United States census serve the researcher well. In Washington, the Library of Congress and the National Archives contain numerous Federal documents and other materials that refer to Gallatin and should not be overlooked.

Index

A

Academy of Geneva, 4
Acme Boot, 91–92
Adult Basic Education Program, 79
African Americans, 26, 31, 53, 69, 82
African Colonization Society, 31
Aintree, 59
Air Force F-4 Fighter Monument, 114, **114**
Air Force F-4 Phantom, 111
Airport Road, 89, 91, 97, 100–101, 104, 106, 110–11
Akron, Ohio, 92
Albert Gallatin Avenue, 112
Albert Gallatin Boulevard, 104, 108, 112
Albright, Edward, 61–62
Albright, Frank, 6
Alexander Funeral Home, 69
Alexander, James, 15–16
Alexander, John, xvi, 10, 23, **10**
Allen, Eliza, 30, 33
Allen, George W., 6, 20
Allen, W.Y., 51
Allen's Restaurant, 63
Allen-Trousdale High School, 50
Alley, L. H., 17
Allied Signal, 97, 110, **108**
Allied Signal Jidosha-Kiki, 110
Allies, 51, 66
Alligator (horse), 59
Allison, Thomas, 17
American Ethnological Society, 5
American La France, 58
American Legion John T. Alexander Post 17, 61, 66, 112, 114
American Revolution. *See* Revolutionary War
American Veterans Memorial, **114**
Anderson, D. B., 17
Anderson, Ed L., 19
Anderson, H. H., 20
Anderson, S. R., 15, **15**
Anderson, Sarah Mac, 71
Anderson's Tobacco Warehouse, 56
Appalachians, 4
Appomattox, 40
Armistice, 51
Armistice Day, 69
Armitage Company, 89
Army, 66
Asia, 66
Atlantic Ocean, 59
Atomic Energy Commision, 84
Auto Club, 49
Avondale, Tenn., 113

B

Bachelor's Hall, 59
Baker, "Aunt" Bettie, 54
Baker, Norval S., 20–21

Baker, Z. W., 16
Bancroft, Bill, 64
Bandy, Max R., 19–20
Bank of Tennessee, 59
Baptist Church, 40, 58, 67
Baptist congregation, 40
Bardstown, Ky., 49
Barker, Henry J., 16, 36
Barker's foundry, 36
Barnes, Alexander, 16
Barry, Ben, 21
Barrymore, 6
Bate, Humphrey, 55
Bate, William B., 42–43, 46, **55**
battle of Chapultepec, 36
battle of Gallatin, 38–39
battle of Nashville, 40
battle of New Orleans, 29
battle of Shiloh, 49
Beatrice Companies, Inc., 83, 100
Beech High School, 112
Beers' 1878 map of Sumner County, **18**
Bell, John, 15
Belote, Donna, v
Belvedere Drive, 97, 110, 112, **72**
Bendix Corporation, 96–97
Bendix-Jidosha Kiki Corporation, 104
Bennett, Dale, v
Berber, A. M., 16
Bethpage, Tenn., 66
Bicentennial Celebration, xv
Big Cheese, **72**
Birmingham, Ala., 59
Black, David, 23
Blackmore, Catherine, 6
Blackmore, F. D., 16–17
Blackmore, J. W., 19, **19**
Blackmore, James A., 15
Blackmore, William M., 15–16, **15**
Blakemore, Polk, 17
Bledsoeborough, 13
Bledsoe Creek, 43, 82
Bledsoe's Lick, 4
Bledsoe's Lick Historical Association, Inc., xvi
Blue, A. M., 19
Blue, W. C., 16–19
Blue Grass Butter, 69
Blue Grass Serenaders, 55
Blythe, S. M., 15
Blythe Street, 40–41, 59, 63, 72, 94
Blythewood, **30**
Board of Aldermen, 26, 40
Board of Trade, 46
Boddie, Elizabeth, 61
Boddie, Rufus, 61
Bosch Breaking Systems, **108**
Boston, Mass., 5
Bowen, H. K., 53

Bowen, John H., 29
Bowen's Lodge No. 21, Knights of Pythias, 45
Bowers, Houston, 17
Bowles, E. Ray, Sr., v
Boyers, Robert M., 15
Boyers, Thomas, 16, 36, 38, **15**
Boyers Street, 50
Bradley, J. G., 21
Bradley, Lucy, v
Branch, J. P., 62
Branham, John M., 52
Bransford, Tenn., 49
Brazil, 36
Briggs, William M., 15–16
Brinkley, Velma, v, xvi
Broadway, 74
Brooks, Monroe, 22
Brooks, Wayne, 23
Brown, C. B., 19
Brown, Clara, 31, **33**
Brown, I. C., 21–22
Brown, J. W., 17
Brown, Nelle Houston, 62
Brown, W. B., 19
Brown, W. H., 17–20, **12**
Browning, Gordon, 69
Brown Milling Company, 60
Brown's Lane, 112
Buchanan, E. O., 19
Buckingham, B. F., 17
Buckingham, T. C., 17
Buckingham, T. L., 17
Buffalo, N.Y., 61–62
Buffalo (hot air ballon), 42, **39**
Bugg, A. D., 15
Bush, George W., 112, 114
Business and Professional Women's Club, 62
Byron's Bar-B-Q, 72, 83, 89, 100–101

C

C. E. Northrup & Sons, 51
Cage's Bend, Tenn., 111
Ca Ira, 4
Cairo, Tenn., 38
Cairo Landing, Tenn., 64
Cairo Road, 76
Caldwell, R. W., 20
Caldwell, Rogers, 59
California, 36, 100
California Industrial Products, 100
Camp Boxwell, 73
Camp Trousdale, 39
Campbell, Everton, v
Canter, Steve, 23
Cantrell, C. C., 17
Cantrell, John M., 19
Carmack, Edward Ward, 45, 82

131

GALLATIN 200

Carman, Tracy, v
Carpenters and Joiners Union, 79
Carthage, Tenn., 30, 33, 56
Caruthers, Bill, 22
Castalian Springs, Tenn., 38, 45
Castle Hall, 45
Central City, Colo., 31
Central City Opera House, 31
Central High School, 50, 52, 54, **54**
Central Powers, 51
Chamber of Commerce, xi, 7, 55, 57, 61–62, 64–65, 70, 112
Champion Fire Extinguisher, 41
Chandler, W. T., 21
Charles C. Parks Company, 92, **72**
Charles Trousdale house, **35**
Charlet, James E., 74
Charlton, Byron, v, 22–23, 100, **22**
Charter Review Committee, 101
Cheney, Dick, 114
Chero-Cola Bottling Plant, 53
Cherokee tribe, 3
Chesapeake and Nashville Railroad Company (C&N), 42–43
Chicago, Ill., 57, 94, 97
Chicago Tribune, 59
Chickasaw tribe, 3
Christian, J. A., 20
Christian Towers, Inc., 85
Christmas festival, 53
Citizen's Blue Ribbon Committee, 101
Citizens Club Calendar, **67**
Civic Improvement League, 47
Civil Rights Act of 1964, 26, 79
Civil War, 3, 5, 13, 38, 40, 110
Clark, Avery, 20
Clark, Isaac, 28
Clark, John, 17
Clark, William, 17
Clark's Miscellany in Prose and Verse, 28
Clearview Park, 69, 91
Clement, Frank, 78
Clifton, Jamie, v
Clinic Bowl, 91, 93, 101, 106
Clinton, William Jefferson, 106
Clinton-Gore inauguration, 108
Clinton High, 107
Cocke, Carroll, 17–19
Coles Bend, Tenn., 70
Cole's ferry, 55
Coles Ferry Road, 6, 104
College Heights Christian Academy, 3, 115
Colorado Society of Pioneers, 31
Colored Knights of Pythias, 53
Columbia, Tenn., 57
Columbian, 29
Commercial Club, 49, 54
Commonwealth Fund of New York City, 65–66
Confederacy, 38
Confederate Army, 38–40
Confederate Cavalry, 39
Confederate monument, **60**
Connecticut, 106
Constitutional Convention, 4
Constitutional Union Party, 38
Cook, Mike, v
Cook, T. J., 19
Cordell Hull Hotel, 67, 76
Corps of Engineers, 72–73, 84, 92, 108, 110
Cosco, 77, 79
Costa Rica, 62
Country Music Association Entertainer of the Year, 91
Country Music World (CMW), 93–94, 97
Cragfont, 28, 97, **31, 113**
Craig, E. B., 20, 63
Craig, Francis, 50, 62
Craig, R. J., 50
Crescent Amusement Company, 62, 72
Cresent Furniture, 70
Cresent Manufacturing Company, 68, 72, 74, 82, 104, 113, **88**
Cresent Wholesale, 70
Crockett, George F., 15–16
Cron, J. E., 19
Cron, R. E., 20

Crump, William H., 17
Crutcher, Hy, 17
Crutcher, J. C., 21
Cuba, 76
Cuban independence, 45
Cumberland Electric Membership Corporation, 72
Cumberland Presbyterian Church, **53**
Cumberland River, ix, 3, 5, 13, 45, 51, 56, 58, 63, 65, 69–72, 110, **57**
Cumberland River Bridge, 55, **79**
Cumberland Telephone and Telegraph Company, 43, 45, 50
Cumberland Telephone Building, **68**
Curtis, Lee, v

D

D. C. Beers and Company, 42
DAB Industries, 89, 96–97
Dalton, O. M., 21
Dark-Fired Tobacco Association Warehouse, 56
David Kregarman Department Store, 53
Day, T. J, 17
DeMeio, Tammy, xvi
Dempsey, Dick, v, 23, **22**
Denver, Colo., 31
Depot Square Shopping Center, 92, 94, **72**
Desha, Robert, 29
Detroit, Mich., 68, 73
Detroit Aluminum Brass, 89
DeWitt, H. H., 18–19
Dillard, J. O., 19
Dismukes, G. R., 18
Ditty, James, 21–22
Dixie Candy Company, 63
Dixon's Creek, 13
Dixon Springs, Tenn., 47–48
Dobbins Pike, 44, 56, 104, 112
Dodson Health Department Building, 112
Dominion Electric Company, 74, 76
Donelson, J. B., 19, **19**
Donelson, John, 13
Donelson, Samuel, 13
Donoho, Charles, 13
Donoho, W. T., 22
DORCO, 83, 86, 100
Dot Records, 70, 72
Dotson, Walter, 19
Douglas Bend, Tenn., 111
Douglas Bend Road, 61
Douglass, C. S., 50
Douglass, Robert G., 15
Dow, Lorenzo, 29
Drane, "Chippy," **63**
Draughon Business College of Nashville, 57
Dresser, Prudence S., 49, 51
Dry Creek, 13
Duke, Lee, 20
Dulin Place, 6
Duncan, D.K., 57
Duncan Street, 101
Durham, J. T., 59
Durham, Robert Neal, 21, 23
Durham, Walter T., v, xvi
Durham Building Supply, 87, 112
Durham Manufacturing Company, 61

E

E. W. Thompson City Park, 70
Eagle Woolen Mills, 40
Earls, A.C., 20
East Franklin Street, 6, 29, 68, 85
Eastland subdivision, 46
East Main Street, 31, 38, 45, 47, 50–51, 54, 58, 61–63, 69–70, 72, 76–78, 84, 86, 89, 100–101, **43, 53, 66, 83**
East Winchester Street, 53
Eaton Corporation, 86, 91, 100
Echols, N. B., 20
Economic and Community Development Committee, 109
Economic Development Agency (EDA), x, 8, 112
Ed Mac Restaurant, 63
Education Improvement Act of 1992, 107
Edwards, Benjamin, 15

Edwards, William H., 16
Edward Ward Carmack Public Library, **93**
Eisenhower, Dwight D., 67
Electoral College, 112
"Electric Light Bonds," 45
Electric Theatre, 47
Elkins, M. S., 17, 19–20
Elliot, William E., 15
Ellis, T. S. ,19
England, ix
Enlow, H. P., 17
Enoch, Paul, 22
Environmental Protection Agency (EPA), 84
Eritech, 107
ESP, 86, 100
Estes Kefauver for President club, 70
Europe, 51, 63
Ewing, J. H., 20
Ewing, M. A., 19
Examiner, 38, 64–65, 74, 78, 89
Examiner-News, 89, 91
Examiner-Tennessean, 52, 62
Exchange Club, 54

F

Factory Lane, 40, 62, 84, 91, 111
Fairest of the Fair, **81**
Fairground Road, 96
Fairvue Plantation, 31, 42, 47, 54, 57, 59, 91, 114, **34**
Farm Bureau, 82
Farmers Loose Leaf Tobacco Warehouse, 52
Federal Food Stamp Program, 80
Federal Housing Administration, 61
Federal troops, 38–39
Federal Works Progess Administration (WPA), 62–63
Fenker, Richard, 22–23
Ferrell, Henry Frank, 23
Ferro Corporation, 85
Fidler, H. R., 19
Finance committee, 8
Finland, 62
Fire Hall, 57
First Amendment, 4
First Amendment Center, 4
First American Corporation of Nashville, 100
First and Peoples National Bank, 53, 100
First and Peoples National Bank Building, 7
First Baptist Church, 38, 45, 69, 86, **43, 47, 83**
First Independent Bank, 104
First Methodist Church *Bulletin*, 65
First Presbyterian Church, 30, **33**
First Tennessee Bank of Memphis, 83
First United Methodist Church, 30, 50, 58, **49**
Fitts, W. J., 96
Fitzgerald, Guy, 57
Fitzgerald, Henry, 40
Fitzgerald House, **46**
Fitzgerald's cotton mill, 40
Fleetwood Homes, 106, **103**
Fletcher, S. J., 48
Fletcher Hotel, 47–48, 50, 60, **61, 64, 76**
Florida, 31
Fly, Felix, 21
Ford, Cortez, 22
Ford and Duke, 56
Ford and Duke Tobacco Warehouse, 52
Forepaugh-Sells Brothers Circus, 49
Formfit Rogers, 97
Fort Donelson, 38
Fort Mackinac, Mich., 39
Fort Street, 63
Fort Thomas, 39–40, **45**
Foster, John B., 16–18
Foster Street, 69, 84
14th U. S. Colored Infantry Regiment, 39
Fowler, Charles, 68
Fowler, Joseph Smith, 40, 44, **44**
Fowler Brothers, 91
Foxland Hall, 52, 61, 93, 100, **36**
Foxland Hall–Country Music World, 97

132

A Time Line History Celebrating the Bicentennial of Gallatin, Tennessee

France, 5
Franklin, B. J., 57
Franklin, Ernest, 18–19
Franklin, Horace E., 20–21
Franklin, Isaac, 31, 33, 54
Franklin, John, 21
Franklin, John C., 20
Franklin, John W., 16
Franklin, Kentucky Boosters, 50
Franklin, Ky., 57
Franklin Milling Company, 57
Franklin Street, 42
Frank Sullivan farm, 60
Freedmen's Bureau, 40
French Revolution, 4
Friendship Hill, 5
Fry, John, 18–20
Fuller, A. N., 20–21
Fulton, D., 15

G

G.P.I. Yearbook 1923, 52
Gaines, Dan, 21
Gallatin
    Airport, 60–61, 63, 89, 97, 111, 114
    Aluminum Products Company, Inc. (GAPCO), 7, 72–73, 77–78, 83, 100, 110, **89**
    and Cairo Turnpike Company, 36
    and Coles Ferry Turnpike, 36
    and Lebanon Railroad Company, 40
    and Ridge Turnpike Company, 33
    Athletic Club, 45
    Aviation Club, 63
    Bicentennial Celebration Committee, Inc., v, xv
    Block Company, 89
    Board of Education, 3, 49–50
    Boat Works, Inc., 82
    Boosters with Chamber of Commerce, 54
    Chamber of Commerce, xv
    Church of Christ, 50, **66**
    City Cemetery, ix–x
    City Council, 8, 10, 14, 26, 46–49, 57, 63, 65–69, 72, 92, 100–101, 104, 106, 110, 112
    City Council Minutes, 17
    City Hall, x, xii, 6, 8, 28, 57, 84–85, 93, **x, 12, 21**
    City Hall Annex, **21**
    City Utilities, **102**
    Civic Center, 101, 104, 109, **14**
    Country Club, 68–70
    Department of Electricity, ix, 80, **21, 92**
    Downtown Merchants Association, xi
    Dry Goods Company, 48
    Electric Power Plant, 45
    Female Academy, 3, 29, 31, 33
    Finance Department, xii, 104
    Fire Department, 55, **xii, 21**
    Green Wave, 93
    Hartsville, and Carthage Turnpike Company, 33
    High School (GHS), 62, 67, 69–70, 83, 89, **75**
    Housing Authority, 73, 91, 97, 112
    Inn, 29
    Junior High School, 78
    Male Seminary, 3
    Milling Company, 57, 60
    Mills (flour), 47
    Municipal Park, xv, 108
    Nashville Interurban, 49
    Natural Gas System, 94
    Park System, 6
    Planning and Codes Department, x
    Planning Commission, x
    Police Department, 84, **9**
    Police Station, **21**
    Post Office, **100**
    Power Plant, 52
    Private Institute (G.P.I.), 3, 52, 54–55
    Public Square, 6, 29, 31, 33, 40, 43–55, 62–64, 67, 78, 83–84, 93, 97, 107, **vi, xiv, 44, 59**
    Public Utilities Department, ix
    Public Works Department, x
    Recorder and City Judge, 9

Rotary Club, 53, 67
    Senior High School, 6, 9, 84–85, 91, 97, 100–101, 106–8, 112, **95**
    Spoke Works, 45
    Steam Plant, 73, 86, 110, 113
    Tennessee Bank, 29
    Turnpike, 33
    Turnpike Company, 31
    TVA Fossil Plant, xvi, **5, 86–87**
    Utilities Office: Gas, Water Sewer, **106**
    Waterworks, **104**
Gallatin, Abraham Alfonse Albert, 4–5, **ii, 29**
Gallatin, Jean, 4
Gallatin-Rolaz, Mme., 4
GAP, 111–12, 115, **107**
Garrott, John, v, xvi, **22**
Garrott, Tommy, v, 23
Garrott Brothers, **104**
Gary Company, 7, 76, 80, 83, 104, 106
Gasskill, D. C., 15
Gemco Electric Plant, 89
General Assembly, 29, 68
General Sessions Court, 82–83
General Shoe Corporation, 64, 66–67, 69, 71, 111, **64, 76**
Genesco, 6–7, 76–77, 79–80, 84, 86, 91, 111
Geneva, Switzerland, 4
Gentlemen's Shakespeare Club, 47
George, H. T., 16
Germany, 50
GF Office Furniture, 87, 92, 94, 101, 111, **99**
Giles, C. D., 70–71
Gillespie Oil Corporation, 54
Glangesia (horse), 60
Glasgow, Ky., 49
Globe Business Furniture, 7, 86, 110
Good Neighbor Mission, 94
Gore, Albert, Jr., 106, 108, 112, 114
Gore, Albert, Sr., 69
Grand Ole Opry, 55
Grant, Ulysses S., 40
Grasslands, 59–60, **73**
Grasslands Hunting and Racing Foundation, 57
Graves, Jo Ann, 112
Gray, Benjamin, 15
Gray, G. S., 16
Gray, L. H., 18
Gray Street, 52, 60
Great Britain, 3, 5, 28
Great Depression, 5, 71
Greater Gallatin, Inc., xi, 7, 93, 100, 110
Greater Nashville Regional Council, 112
Great Highway from the Lakes to the Gulf, 47
Great Lakes, 115
Green, Reuben D., 15
Greenville, S. C., 83
Green Wave Drive, 110, 112
Greenwood Apartment Complex, 112
Guardian, 31
Guild, Joan, 63
Guild, Josephus Conn, 6, 15, 35, 39
Guild, Lewis, 69
Guild, Mrs. Lewis, 69
Guildwood, 6
Gulf of Mexico, 115
Guthrie, George N., 17–19, **19**
Guthrie, Robert T., 20–21
Guthrie Building, 7

H

H. E. Franklin and Sons Machine Shop, 68
Habitat for Humanity, 26, 110
Hadley, William, 12, 15, **12**
Halewood Homeowners Association, 101
Hall, John, 29
Hall, William, 29, 31, **34**
Hallum, Robert, 17
Hamilton-Cosco, Inc., 7, 74, 87
Hampton, Randy, 23
Hancock, John, v, 23, **22**
Hancock Street, 101, 109
Handicapped Adult Training Services, 93

Harper, Cora, xvi
Harper, Ellis, 40
Harpole, A. W., 21
Harris, Isaac W., Jr., 17–18
Harris, John, 20
Harris, John R., 20
Harris, Peggy, 22
Harris Lane, 112
Harrison, J. A., 20
Harrison Barracks, **37**
Harsh, Nathan, xvi
Hart, D. P., 16–18
Hart Street, 112
Hartsville, Tenn., 33, 43, 46, 55, 59, 83–85, 91, 97
Hartsville Pike, 6, 38, 52, 79, 89, 97
Havre, Mont., 62
Hawkins, C. E., 45
Hawkins Preparatory School, 3, 6, 45, 49, 51–52, 57, 60
Hayes, Craig, xvi, 10, 23, **10**
Haynes, Allen, xvi
Haynie, X. B., 18
Head, Charles R., 41
Head Start, 79
Health Officer, 63
Hendersonville, Tenn., 7, 70–72, 83, 87, 91, 100, 111–12
Henley, Miles, B., 17
Henley, W. B., 17
Henley, William, 16
Henley, W. J., 17
Hermans, S., 17
Hermitage Hotel WSM-NBC orchestra, 62
Hewgley, C. E., 20
Hickman, E. F., 20
Highway 109, 6, 72, 79, 94, 101, 104, 107, 111, **79**
Highway 109 Bypass, 6, 101, 104, 108, 110
Hill-Burton Act, 73
Historical Cragfont, Inc., xvi
Hite, L. W., 20
Hitler, Adolf, 63
Hix, B. H., 19–20
Hix, Harold, 20
Hoeganaes Corporation, 87, 89, 96, 111, **109**
Holder, Harry, A., 20
Holt, Daryl, xvi, 10, 23, **11**
Homecoming '86, 100
Hooper, Hal, 22
Horine, George, 57
Horn, Joab, 16
Hotel Sumner, 42, **50**
House, A. E., 19
House, E. B. "Rabbit," 12, 20, **12**
House, James, 17
House, R. E., 19
House of Representatives, 4
Houston, Sam, 30, 33
Hovenden, Phyllis, 23
Howard, B. R., 16
Howard, J. E., 17
Howard Elementary School, 6, 60, 67, 87, 89
Howard Female College, 3, 6, 38, 40–42, 49–50, 55, 57, 60, **52**
Howard Lodge, No. 13, International Organization of Odd Fellows, 35
Hunter, Frank, 20
Hunter, Jim, 23
Hurt, Kay, v
Hutchings, John, 28

I

Idlewild, 64
ILS Navigational System, 100
Indianapolis, Ind., 48
Industrial Development Association, 70
Industrial Development Board, 109, 112
Industrial Park, 106–7, 110
Infact Corporation, 110
Ingram, Walter Aurelius, 49
International Steeplechase, 59
Interstate 840, 109
Interstate 40, 6, 79
Interstate Homes, Inc., 101

GALLATIN 200

Interurban Railway, 7, 46, 50, 56, **62, 71**
Iran, 92
Isaac Bledsoe's Fort, 52, 108
Isaac Franklin Institute, 33
Itta Bena, 69

J

J. A. Sloan Company, 57, **72**
J. W. Walton Flouring Mills, 41
Jackson, Andrew, 13, 28–31
Jackson, Harold, 23
Jackson, Rachel, 13
Jackson and Hutchings, 28
Jackson Highway, 52, 54, 60
Jamison Bedding, 100
Japan, 65–66
Japanese troops, 64
Jarman, James Franklin, 71
Jarman, Maxey, 71
Jarman Shoe Company, 60, 62, 111
Jaycees, 67
Jefferson, Thomas, 5, 28
Jeffries, James J., 48
Jeffries-Johnson, 48
Jemison, B. F., 17
Jockey Club, 29
John Bell Brown residence, 6
Johnson, Andrew, 39–40
Johnson, Columbus, 17
Johnson, Jack, 48
Johnson, James S., 16
Johnson, James W., 16
Johnson, R. W., 38–39
Johnson, Townes B., 22
Jo Horton Fall, **57**
Joint Resolutions of the General Assembly, **xii**
Jones, E. T., 20
Jones, Ellis, 72, 74
Jones, R. M., 19
Jones Hotel, 48
Jones Livery Company, 68
Jones Street, 80
Joslin Street, 101
Journal, 31
Joyner, W. H., 19

K

Keen, W. M., 19
Keen Broom Factory, 57
Kelly, F. A., Jr., 20
Kelly, Fred A., III, v, 22, **20, 22**
Kemp, Anne, 23
Kemp, Ottis, 21–22, **20**
Kennedy, John F., 76
Kentucky, 43, 49, 54
Kentucky-Tennessee Light and Power Company, 57, 62–63
Key, Hilary W., 17, 40, **45**
Key Stewart Methodist Episcopal Church, **48**
Keystone Hotel, 54
King, C. B., 16–17
King, Samuel, 42
King, Thomas H., 17–18
King of Spain, 59–60
King Solomon Lodge No. 94, F.&A.M., 33
King Solomon Lodge of F.&A.M., No. 6 of 1808, 28, 33
Kirkpatrick, Bill, v
Kittrell, Bruce, 23
Kittrell, Connie, xvi, 9, 14, 23, **10**
Kittrell, Jack, 22
Kittrell, Rutledge, 21
Knight, John W., 18
Knight, William C., 16
Knights of Pythias, 44
Kop Ron Machine Company, 73
Korean War, 5, 70
Kraft Cheese Company, 57, 60, 69, 74, 76, 94, **72**

L

L&N Depot, 54, 57, 82, 92
L&N Depot Tower, 64
L&N Railroad, 6, 55, 60, 63
L&N Steam Locomotive, **74**
Lackey, Sam E., 20
Lackey, W. N., 12, 59, 63, **12, 61**
Lambuth Methodist Church, 68
Langley Hall, 6, 67
Lanier, Mannie, 53
Lankford, Robert W., v, 23, **22**
Lassiter, F. H., 44
Lauk, J. F., 17
Lawson, J. H., 71
Lea, Robert, xvi, 10, 23, **11**
Leavenworth, Kans., 31
Lebanon, Tenn., 7, 110
LECO Corporation, 100
Lee, Robert E., 40
Legion's Southeastern Regional Championship, 112
Legion World Series, 112
Lewis, Charles, 15
Lexington, Ky., 57
Linatex Corporation of America, 106
Lincoln, Abraham, 38–40
Lincoln farm, 49
Lions Club, 67
Lions International, 62
Local Industrial Development Association, 70
Lock Four Road, 109
London, England, ix, 4, 64
Long, Elisha, 29
Long Hollow Golf Course, x, 8
Long Hollow Pike, 11, 87, 92, 97
Long Hollow Turnpike Company, 36
Los Angeles, Calif., 72
Louisville, Ky., 49
Louisville & Nashville Railroad (L&N), 36, 38, 42, 46, 89
Love, B. E., 19
Love, George, 15–16
Loveless Hospital, 70
Lower Station Camp Creek Road, 109
Lyles, Fount, 21
Lyon, Samuel, 18–19
Lyon Street, 57

M

Machinists Union, 79
Maddox, H. H., 21
Maddox, Howard, 22
Maddox, J. L., 20
Maddox, Johnny, 70
Maddox, Robert, 21
Madison, James, 5
Main Post Office, 96
Main Street, 7, 30, 33, 35, 43–44, 93, **vi**
Main Street High School, 47–48
Main Street Program, 100
Main Street School, 43
Malone, Deotha J., xvi, 9, 22–23, **10**
Malone, John H., 16
Malone, Yvonne, 23
Mandrell, Barbara, 91
Mansker's Creek, 56
Mansker's Fort, 4
Maple Street, 72, 96, 100, 104, 106, 112–13, **88**
Maple Valley, 6
Marcar Transportation, 110
Martha White Industries, 83
Mattox, E. G., 21–23
Mayberry, Ed, xvi, 11, 23, **11**
Mayor and Sanitary Committee, 42
Mayor's Honorary Committee, v
McAlister, Hill, 60
McCord, Jim, 68
McCormick, J. W., 19
McCormick, Robert, 59
McDonald, Cordell, 22, **20**
McDonald, Ed., 21–22
McGinn, J. B., 58
McKinley, T., 17
McKoin, Daniel T., 16
McLean, William, 21
McQuiddy, H. C., 17
McVaw, D., 17
McWherter, Ned, 114
Melvin, Russ, 23
Memphis, Tenn., 29
Mentlo, James A., 17
Mercury Development Company, 64
Metcalf, Jerry, 22
Metro (Nashville), 7
Mexican War, 5
Mexican War Monument, 36, **39**
Mexico, 36
Michigan, 100
Middle and East Tennessee Central Railroad, 43
Middle Tennessee Council Boy Scouts of America, 73
Middle Tennessee Medical Association, 49
Middle Tennessee State Fair, 38
Middle Tennessee State Normal College, 3, 47
Middle Tennessee State University (MTSU), 47
Midwest, 68
Milliken, Glenda, v, xvi
Minnetonka, 59
Minnich, Dan, 62
Minor, J. V., 17
Mississippi Vocational College, 69
Mitchell, G. W., 20
Mitchell, John, 29
Mitchellville, Tenn., 59
Montgomery, W. G., 18
Montgomery, W. N., 16
Moore, R. E., 17
Moore, Robert N., 70
Moore, W. C., 16
Moore, William, 16–17
Morgan, Bob, v
Morgan, John Hunt, 38–39
Morrison Street, 67–68
Motley, Willis, 17
Mudd, Reggie, v
Muddy Run, 6
Multimedia, Inc., 83, 89
Munday, W. S., 17
Municipal Gold Course, 97
Murfreesboro, Tenn., 73
Murray, Thomas, 13
Murrey, J. W., 20
Musical Observer, 49

N

Naive, J. J., 19
Nashville, ix, 7, 33, 35, 39–40, 42, 45, 48–49, 51–52, 60, 62, 65, 70, 72, 83, 100, 110, 115
Nashville-Gallatin Interurban, 51
Nashville-Gallatin Turnpike, 49
Nashville Gas Company, 94
Nashville Pike, 6, 11, 56, 59, 61, 82–83, 92, 96, 100–101, 109
Nashville Symphony, 97
Nashville Vols, 52
Natcher, Joseph, 16
Natchez, Miss., 29
National Association for the Advancement of Colored People (NAACP), 82
National Broadcasting Company (NBC), 50
National Chamber of Commerce, 64
National Drive, 89
National Guard, 70
National Guard Armory, 70, 100
National Historic Landmark, 5
National Park Service of the Department of the Interior, 5, 91
National Register of Historic Places, 97
National Trust for Historic Preservation, 93
Native Americans, 5
Neal, R. L., 21
Needles, J. H., 17
Neophogen College, 41–42
New Guild Elementary School, 72
News-Examiner, 83, 89, 92
New York, N. Y., 36, 49, 114
New York state, 5
Nichols Lane, 84
Nicholson, Samuel, 17
Nickelson, Jonas, 16–17, 36

134

A Time Line History Celebrating the Bicentennial of Gallatin, Tennessee

France, 5
Franklin, B. J., 57
Franklin, Ernest, 18–19
Franklin, Horace E., 20–21
Franklin, Isaac, 31, 33, 54
Franklin, John, 21
Franklin, John C., 20
Franklin, John W., 16
Franklin, Kentucky Boosters, 50
Franklin, Ky., 57
Franklin Milling Company, 57
Franklin Street, 42
Frank Sullivan farm, 60
Freedmen's Bureau, 40
French Revolution, 4
Friendship Hill, 5
Fry, John, 18–20
Fuller, A. N., 20–21
Fulton, D., 15

G

G.P.I. Yearbook 1923, 52
Gaines, Dan, 21
Gallatin
    Airport, 60–61, 63, 89, 97, 111, 114
    Aluminum Products Company, Inc. (GAPCO), 7, 72–73,
        77–78, 83, 100, 110, **89**
    and Cairo Turnpike Company, 36
    and Coles Ferry Turnpike, 36
    and Lebanon Railroad Company, 40
    and Ridge Turnpike Company, 33
    Atheletic Club, 45
    Aviation Club, 63
    Bicentennial Celebration Committee, Inc., v, xv
    Block Company, 89
    Board of Education, 3, 49–50
    Boat Works, Inc., 82
    Boosters with Chamber of Commerce, 54
    Chamber of Commerce, xv
    Church of Christ, 50, **66**
    City Cemetery, ix–x
    City Council, 8, 10, 14, 26, 46–49, 57, 63, 65–69, 72, 92,
        100–101, 104, 106, 110, 112
    City Council Minutes, 17
    City Hall, x, xii, 6, 8, 28, 57, 84–85, 93, **x, 12, 21**
    City Hall Annex, **21**
    City Utilities, **102**
    Civic Center, 101, 104, 109, **14**
    Country Club, 68–70
    Department of Electricity, ix, 80, **21, 92**
    Downtown Merchants Association, xi
    Dry Goods Company, 48
    Electric Power Plant, 45
    Female Academy, 3, 29, 31, 33
    Finance Department, xii, 104
    Fire Department, 55, **xii, 21**
    Green Wave, 93
    Hartsville, and Carthage Turnpike Company, 33
    High School (GHS), 62, 67, 69–70, 83, 89, **75**
    Housing Authority, 73, 91, 97, 112
    Inn, 29
    Junior High School, 78
    Male Seminary, 3
    Milling Company, 57, 60
    Mills (flour), 47
    Municipal Park, xv, 108
    Nashville Interurban, 49
    Natural Gas System, 94
    Park System, 6
    Planning and Codes Department, x
    Planning Commission, x
    Police Department, 84, **9**
    Police Station, **21**
    Post Office, **100**
    Power Plant, 52
    Private Institute (G.P.I.), 3, 52, 54–55
    Public Square, 6, 29, 31, 33, 40, 43–55, 62–64, 67, 78, 83–84,
        93, 97, 107, **vi, xiv, 44, 59**
    Public Utilities Department, ix
    Public Works Department, x
    Recorder and City Judge, 9

Rotary Club, 53, 67
Senior High School, 6, 9, 84–85, 91, 97, 100–101, 106–8, 112,
    95
Spoke Works, 45
Steam Plant, 73, 86, 110, 113
Tennessee Bank, 29
Turnpike, 33
Turnpike Company, 31
TVA Fossil Plant, xvi, **5, 86–87**
Utilities Office: Gas, Water Sewer, **106**
Waterworks, **104**
Gallatin, Abraham Alfonse Albert, 4–5, **ii, 29**
Gallatin, Jean, 4
Gallatin–Rolaz, Mme., 4
GAP, 111–12, 115, **107**
Garrott, John, v, xvi, **22**
Garrott, Tommy, v, 23
Garrott Brothers, **104**
Gary Company, 7, 76, 80, 83, 104, 106
Gasskill, D. C., 15
Gemco Electric Plant, 89
General Assembly, 29, 68
General Sessions Court, 82–83
General Shoe Corporation, 64, 66–67, 69, 71, 111, **64, 76**
Genesco, 6–7, 76–77, 79–80, 84, 86, 91, 111
Geneva, Switzerland, 4
Gentlemen's Shakespeare Club, 47
George, H. T., 16
Germany, 50
GF Office Furniture, 87, 92, 94, 101, 111, **99**
Giles, C. D., 70–71
Gillespie Oil Corporation, 54
Glangesia (horse), 60
Glasgow, Ky., 49
Globe Business Furniture, 7, 86, 110
Good Neighbor Mission, 94
Gore, Albert, Jr., 106, 108, 112, 114
Gore, Albert, Sr., 69
Grand Ole Opry, 55
Grant, Ulysses S., 40
Grasslands, 59–60, **73**
Grasslands Hunting and Racing Foundation, 57
Graves, Jo Ann, 112
Gray, Benjamin, 15
Gray, G. S., 16
Gray, L. H., 18
Gray Street, 52, 60
Great Britain, 3, 5, 28
Great Depression, 5, 71
Greater Gallatin, Inc., xi, 7, 93, 100, 110
Greater Nashville Regional Council, 112
Great Highway from the Lakes to the Gulf, 47
Great Lakes, 115
Green, Reuben D., 15
Greenville, S. C., 83
Green Wave Drive, 110, 112
Greenwood Apartment Complex, 112
Guardian, 31
Guild, Joan, 63
Guild, Josephus Conn, 6, 15, 35, 39
Guild, Lewis, 69
Guild, Mrs. Lewis, 69
Guildwood, 6
Gulf of Mexico, 115
Guthrie, George N., 17–19, **19**
Guthrie, Robert T., 20–21
Guthrie Building, 7

H

H. E. Franklin and Sons Machine Shop, 68
Habitat for Humanity, 26, 110
Hadley, William, 12, 15, **12**
Halewood Homeowners Association, 101
Hall, John, 29
Hall, William, 29, 31, **34**
Hallum, Robert, 17
Hamilton-Cosco, Inc., 7, 74, 87
Hampton, Randy, 23
Hancock, John, v, 23, **22**
Hancock Street, 101, 109
Handicapped Adult Training Services, 93

Harper, Cora, xvi
Harper, Ellis, 40
Harpole, A. W., 21
Harris, Isaac W., Jr., 17–18
Harris, John, 20
Harris, John R., 20
Harris, Peggy, 22
Harris Lane, 112
Harrison, J. A., 20
Harrison Barracks, **37**
Harsh, Nathan, xvi
Hart, D. P., 16–18
Hart Street, 112
Hartsville, Tenn., 33, 43, 46, 55, 59, 83–85, 91, 97
Hartsville Pike, 6, 38, 52, 79, 89, 97
Havre, Mont., 62
Hawkins, C. E., 45
Hawkins Preparatory School, 3, 6, 45, 49, 51–52, 57, 60
Hayes, Craig, xvi, 10, 23, **10**
Haynes, Allen, xvi
Haynie, X. B., 18
Head, Charles R., 41
Head Start, 79
Health Officer, 63
Hendersonville, Tenn., 7, 70–72, 83, 87, 91, 100, 111–12
Henley, Miles, B., 17
Henley, W. B., 17
Henley, William, 16
Henley, W. J., 17
Hermans, S., 17
Hermitage Hotel WSM–NBC orchestra, 62
Hewgley, C. E., 20
Hickman, E. F., 20
Highway 109, 6, 72, 79, 94, 101, 104, 107, 111, **79**
Highway 109 Bypass, 6, 101, 104, 108, 110
Hill–Burton Act, 73
Historical Cragfont, Inc., xvi
Hite, L. W., 20
Hitler, Adolf, 63
Hix, B. H., 19–20
Hix, Harold, 20
Hoeganaes Corporation, 87, 89, 96, 111, **109**
Holder, Harry, A., 20
Holt, Daryl, xvi, 10, 23, **11**
Homecoming '86, 100
Hooper, Hal, 22
Horine, George, 57
Horn, Joab, 16
Hotel Sumner, 42, **50**
House, A. E., 19
House, E. B. "Rabbit," 12, 20, **12**
House, James, 17
House, R. E., 19
House of Representatives, 4
Houston, Sam, 30, 33
Hovenden, Phyllis, 23
Howard, B. R., 16
Howard, J. E., 17
Howard Elementary School, 6, 60, 67, 87, 89
Howard Female College, 3, 6, 38, 40–42, 49–50, 55, 57, 60,
    52
Howard Lodge, No. 13, International Organization of Odd
    Fellows, 35
Hunter, Frank, 20
Hunter, Jim, 23
Hurt, Kay, v
Hutchings, John, 28

I

Idlewild, 64
ILS Navigational System, 100
Indianapolis, Ind., 48
Industrial Development Association, 70
Industrial Development Board, 109, 112
Industrial Park, 106–7, 110
Infact Corporation, 110
Ingram, Walter Aurelius, 49
International Steeplechase, 59
Interstate 840, 109
Interstate 40, 6, 79
Interstate Homes, Inc., 101

133

GALLATIN 200

Interurban Railway, 7, 46, 50, 56, **62, 71**
Iran, 92
Isaac Bledsoe's Fort, 52, 108
Isaac Franklin Institute, 33
Itta Bena, 69

J

J. A. Sloan Company, 57, **72**
J. W. Walton Flouring Mills, 41
Jackson, Andrew, 13, 28–31
Jackson, Harold, 23
Jackson, Rachel, 13
Jackson and Hutchings, 28
Jackson Highway, 52, 54, 60
Jamison Bedding, 100
Japan, 65–66
Japanese troops, 64
Jarman, James Franklin, 71
Jarman, Maxey, 71
Jarman Shoe Company, 60, 62, 111
Jaycees, 67
Jefferson, Thomas, 5, 28
Jeffries, James J., 48
Jeffries-Johnson, 48
Jemison, B. F., 17
Jockey Club, 29
John Bell Brown residence, 6
Johnson, Andrew, 39–40
Johnson, Columbus, 17
Johnson, Jack, 48
Johnson, James S., 16
Johnson, James W., 16
Johnson, R. W., 38–39
Johnson, Townes B., 22
Jo Horton Fall, **57**
Joint Resolutions of the General Assembly, **xii**
Jones, E. T., 20
Jones, Ellis, 72, 74
Jones, R. M., 19
Jones Hotel, 48
Jones Livery Company, 68
Jones Street, 80
Joslin Street, 101
Journal, 31
Joyner, W. H., 19

K

Keen, W. M., 19
Keen Broom Factory, 57
Kelly, F. A., Jr., 20
Kelly, Fred A., III, v, 22, **20, 22**
Kemp, Anne, 23
Kemp, Ottis, 21–22, **20**
Kennedy, John F., 76
Kentucky, 43, 49, 54
Kentucky-Tennessee Light and Power Company, 57, 62–63
Key, Hilary W., 17, 40, **45**
Key Stewart Methodist Episcopal Church, **48**
Keystone Hotel, 54
King, C. B., 16–17
King, Samuel, 42
King, Thomas H., 17–18
King of Spain, 59–60
King Solomon Lodge No. 94, F.&A.M., 33
King Solomon Lodge of F.&A.M., No. 6 of 1808, 28, 33
Kirkpatrick, Bill, v
Kittrell, Bruce, 23
Kittrell, Connie, xvi, 9, 14, 23, **10**
Kittrell, Jack, 22
Kittrell, Rutledge, 21
Knight, John W., 18
Knight, William C., 16
Knights of Pythias, 44
Kop Ron Machine Company, 73
Korean War, 5, 70
Kraft Cheese Company, 57, 60, 69, 74, 76, 94, **72**

L

L&N Depot, 54, 57, 82, 92
L&N Depot Tower, 64

L&N Railroad, 6, 55, 60, 63
L&N Steam Locomotive, **74**
Lackey, Sam E., 20
Lackey, W. N., 12, 59, 63, **12, 61**
Lambuth Methodist Church, 68
Langley Hall, 6, 67
Lanier, Mannie, 53
Lankford, Robert W., v, 23, **22**
Lassiter, F. H., 44
Lauk, J. F., 17
Lawson, J. H., 71
Lea, Robert, xvi, 10, 23, **11**
Leavenworth, Kans., 31
Lebanon, Tenn., 7, 110
LECO Corporation, 100
Lee, Robert E., 40
Legion's Southeastern Regional Championship, 112
Legion World Series, 112
Lewis, Charles, 15
Lexington, Ky., 57
Linatex Corporation of America, 106
Lincoln, Abraham, 38–40
Lincoln farm, 49
Lions Club, 67
Lions International, 62
Local Industrial Development Association, 70
Lock Four Road, 109
London, England, ix, 4, 64
Long, Elisha, 29
Long Hollow Golf Course, x, 8
Long Hollow Pike, 11, 87, 92, 97
Long Hollow Turnpike Company, 36
Los Angeles, Calif., 72
Louisville, Ky., 49
Louisville & Nashville Railroad (L&N), 36, 38, 42, 46, 89
Love, B. E., 19
Love, George, 15–16
Loveless Hospital, 70
Lower Station Camp Creek Road, 109
Lyles, Fount, 21
Lyon, Samuel, 18–19
Lyon Street, 57

M

Machinists Union, 79
Maddox, H. H., 21
Maddox, Howard, 22
Maddox, J. L., 20
Maddox, Johnny, 70
Maddox, Robert, 21
Madison, James, 5
Main Post Office, 96
Main Street, 7, 30, 33, 35, 43–44, 93, **vi**
Main Street High School, 47–48
Main Street Program, 100
Main Street School, 43
Malone, Deotha J., xvi, 9, 22–23, **10**
Malone, John H., 16
Malone, Yvonne, 23
Mandrell, Barbara, 91
Mansker's Creek, 56
Mansker's Fort, 4
Maple Street, 72, 96, 100, 104, 106, 112–13, **88**
Maple Valley, 6
Marcar Transportation, 110
Martha White Industries, 83
Mattox, E. G., 21–23
Mayberry, Ed, xvi, 11, 23, **11**
Mayor and Sanitary Committee, 42
Mayor's Honorary Committee, v
McAlister, Hill, 60
McCord, Jim, 68
McCormick, J. W., 19
McCormick, Robert, 59
McDonald, Cordell, 22, **20**
McDonald, Ed., 21–22
McGinn, J. B., 58
McKinley, T., 17
McKoin, Daniel T., 16
McLean, William, 21
McQuiddy, H. C., 17

McVaw, D., 17
McWherter, Ned, 114
Melvin, Russ, 23
Memphis, Tenn., 29
Mentlo, James A., 17
Mercury Development Company, 64
Metcalf, Jerry, 22
Metro (Nashville), 7
Mexican War, 5
Mexican War Monument, 36, **39**
Mexico, 36
Michigan, 100
Middle and East Tennessee Central Railroad, 43
Middle Tennessee Council Boy Scouts of America, 73
Middle Tennessee Medical Association, 49
Middle Tennessee State Fair, 38
Middle Tennessee State Normal College, 3, 47
Middle Tennessee State University (MTSU), 47
Midwest, 68
Milliken, Glenda, v, xvi
Minnetonka, 59
Minnich, Dan, 62
Minor, J. V., 17
Mississippi Vocational College, 69
Mitchell, G. W., 20
Mitchell, John, 29
Mitchellville, Tenn., 59
Montgomery, W. G., 18
Montgomery, W. N., 16
Moore, R. E., 17
Moore, Robert N., 70
Moore, W. C., 16
Moore, William, 16–17
Morgan, Bob, v
Morgan, John Hunt, 38–39
Morrison Street, 67–68
Motley, Willis, 17
Mudd, Reggie, v
Muddy Run, 6
Multimedia, Inc., 83, 89
Munday, W. S., 17
Municipal Gold Course, 97
Murfreesboro, Tenn., 73
Murray, Thomas, 13
Murrey, J. W., 20
Musical Observer, 49

N

Naive, J. J., 19
Nashville, ix, 7, 33, 35, 39–40, 42, 45, 48–49, 51–52, 60, 62, 65, 70, 72, 83, 100, 110, 115
Nashville-Gallatin Interurban, 51
Nashville-Gallatin Turnpike, 49
Nashville Gas Company, 94
Nashville Pike, 6, 11, 56, 59, 61, 82–83, 92, 96, 100–101, 109
Nashville Symphony, 97
Nashville Vols, 52
Natcher, Joseph, 16
Natchez, Miss., 29
National Association for the Advancement of Colored People (NAACP), 82
National Broadcasting Company (NBC), 50
National Chamber of Commerce, 64
National Drive, 89
National Guard, 70
National Guard Armory, 70, 100
National Historic Landmark, 5
National Park Service of the Department of the Interior, 5, 91
National Register of Historic Places, 97
National Trust for Historic Preservation, 93
Native Americans, 5
Neal, R. L., 21
Needles, J. H., 17
Neophogen College, 41–42
New Guild Elementary School, 72
News-Examiner, 83, 89, 92
New York, N.Y., 36, 49, 114
New York state, 5
Nichols Lane, 84
Nicholson, Samuel, 17
Nickelson, Jonas, 16–17, 36

134

A Time Line History Celebrating the Bicentennial of Gallatin, Tennessee

1924 Almanac, **12**
North Belvedere, 89, 92, 96, 101
North Boyers Avenue, 82
North Carolina, 3–4, 107
North Carolina Land Grant No. 1, 4
North Water Street, 6, 47–48, 53–4, 59, 63, 67–69, 114
Number One, Tenn., 56
Nye, Shadrack, 13

O

O'Dell, J. C., 19
Oakland, **41**
Oakley, **42**
Octagon House, 6
Octoberfest, 93
Odd Fellows Hall, 38
Odom, Peter, v
Odom's Bend Road, 71–72
Offitt, George, Sr., v
Offitt's Coronet Band, 49
Ohio, 100
Oldham, W. L., 19
Old Hickory, Tenn., 5
Old Hickory Dam, 72
Old Hickory Lake, 5, 27, 72–73, 84, **89–90, 97**
Old Highway 109 North, 89
Old Race Track Grounds, 42
101st U. S. Colored Infantry, 40
Organization of Petroleum Exporting Countries (OPEC), 91
Orman, H., 19–20
Outlaw, Fred., 20–21
Owen, U. J., 62
Owen's Tobacco Factory, 65
Owen Tobacco Works of Eagleville, 62

P

Pacific and Asian War, 66
Paine, Eleazor, 39
Palace Theater, 55, 66–67, 110, **70**
Paramount Records, 72
Pardue, W. W., 19
Parker-Bath Ltd., 101
Parks, Charles C., 57
Parsons, David, v
Patton, George S., 63, 65
Peach Valley, Tenn., 54
Peacock, James, 17, **15**
Pearl Harbor, 64
Pennsylvania, 4–5
Pentagon, 114
Perdue, Hub, 52
Pericles Academy, 29
Perkins, C. E., 20
Perkins, Tommy, v
Perkins Drug Store, 45
Perry, Paul, xvi, 11, 23, **11**
Persian Gulf War, 5, 104
Person, E. E., 20
Person, H. W., 48
Person, J. R., 19–20
Peytona, Tenn., 66
Peyton, Balie, 31, 35–36, 38–39
Peyton, Balie, Jr., 39
Peyton, Joseph H., 35–36
Peyton's Stakes, 35
Philadelphia Cream Cheese, 60
Philadelphia Exposition, 42
Phillips, I. N., 17
Pilot Knob Hill, 59, 76–77
Polk, James K., 35
Porter, Charles, 17
Portland, Tenn., 7, 39, 111
Possum Hunters, 55
Powell, C. E., 19
Presidential Award for Excellence in Science and Mathematics, 108, 113
President's Ball, 62
Price and Day Stagecoach, **58**
Prince, Nat, 15
Prince, William, 15

Public Health Nursing Service, 59
Public Safety Committee, 8
Public Service Committee, 8
Pumping Station Road, 83
Puryear, W. P., Jr., 21, **20**
Pythian College, 43–44, **55**

R

R. C. Owen Tobacco Company, 59, 62, 67, **76, 80**
R. R. Donnelley and Sons, 84–85, 91, **96**
Radicals, 40
Radical Unionists, 40
Railroad Avenue, 40, 43, 48, 51, 54–55
Ralph Rogers Company, 71–72, 76–77
Ramer, Hal R., 82
Ramsey, R. T., 19
Randolph, David, v
Randy's Record Shop, 68–69, 72, 104, **84**
Ran-Wood Production, 82
Rappahannock Wire Co., 106
Read, Charles, 47
Read, Opie, 52, 94
Rebels, 39
Rebound, Inc., 100, 112
Recreation Centers, 64
Red Cross, 114
Red Devils, 62
Red Fox, (Sioux chief), 52
Redman Building Products, 83
Redman Industries, 83
Red River, 60, 68
Red River Road, 6, 39, 47, 58, 60, 63, 91
Red River Turnpike Company, 33
Reed, Charles, 42, 44
Reimer, Tom, 62
Reno, Nev., 48
Revolutionary War, 3, 4
Rich Products Corporation, 101, **103**
Ring, Baker, 23
Ring, Levy, **37**
Robert Bosch Group, 110
Robert M. Boyers Building, 100, **29**
Robert M. Boyers House, **34**
Robert Moore General Hospital, 70
Robertson, James, 13
Robertson, W. N., 20
Rodemer, J. C., 17
Rogan, Charles B., 57
Rogan, William, 23
Roosevelt, Franklin D., 60–61, 66
Rose Mont, 6, 35, 63, 65, 69, 107, **v**
Rose Mont Renaissance, 6
Rose Mont Restoration Foundation, Inc., xvi, 6
Ross, Ann, xvi
Roth, W. F., 19
Roth Jewelry Store, 56, 110
Rowles, W. P., 15
Roxy Theater, 62, 72, **77**
Rucker-Stewart Middle School, 109–10
Russwurm, J. W., 19
Ruth, John, 23
Rutherford, 4
Rutherford, Griffith, 4
Ryman, Tom, **57**

S

Saffarrans, Daniel, 15
Samsonite, 73
Sanders, Charles G., 15
Sanitation Department, ix
Santa Claus, 12, 53, **12**
Schamberger, W. G., 19, 45, 48–49, **19**
Schamberger Building, 7
Schamberger's, 47
Schell, A. R., 19
Schell, H.A., 6, 16–18
Schell, S.T., 15
Schell, Samuel F., 15–17
Schreiner, David, v, 23, **22**
Scott, Bettye, 22–23

Scottsville, Ky., 46, 49, 55
Scottsville Pike, 38, 69, 78
Seay, Frank, 20–21
Second Army, 63–64
Second International Steeplechase, 60
Secretary of the Treasury, 5
Seigenthaler, John, 4
Seminole War of 1836, 5, 31, 33
Servpro Industries, 100
Shafer Middle School, 112
Shaffer Electric Company, 7, 76, 80, 100
Shaw, Frank, 23
Shaw, Virgil, 21
Shawnee tribe, 3
Shelby, David, 29
Shepherd Products, Inc., 110
Shults, Bobby, 23
Simpson, B. F., 15
Simpson, S. R., 17
Simpson, W. A. J., 19–20
Smith, Baxter, 16
Smith, Harold, 23
Smith, Lee, 20
Smith Street, 31, 82, 91, 94
Solomon, William, 15–16
Southeast, 42, 68
Southern Association of Colleges and Secondary Schools, 52
Southern Bell Telephone and Telegraph Company, 68
Southern Blacking Manufacturing Company, 41
Southern Grasslands Hunt and Racing Foundation, 59
Southern Methodists, 41
South Street School, 43
South Tunnel, 40, 55
South Water Street, 6–7, 31, 54, 60, 63, 66, 68, 70, 72, 82, 93, 100
Spain, 45
Spanish American War, 5, **63**
Spencer's Flour Mills, 36
Spillers, D. K., 17–19
Sporer, F. A., 16
Springfield, Tenn., 48
St. Blaise (horse), 44
St. Charles, Joe, 21
St. John Vianney Catholic Church, 59, 69, 114, 115
St. John Vianney School, **94**
Staley, Oscar, 15
Stamford, Conn., 70
Stark, E. M., 20–21
Starr, Louis M., 64
Station Camp Creek, 111
Station Camp Creek Road, 89, 91, 112
Steam Plant Road, 84, 100, 107
Strother, Robert, 17
Stuart, Vena, 68
Suddarth, Thomas, 22
Suddarth Phonograph Company, 51
Sumner Academy, 3, 83, 115, **95**
Sumner Armory, 39
Sumner Auto Club, 52
Sumner Canning Company, 54
Sumner Cotton Manufacturing Company, **56**
Sumner County, ix, xv, xvi, 4, 35, 42, 51–53, 55, 62, 66, 78, 82, 91, 93, 109
    Administration Building, 101, **110–11, 102**
    Agricultural Society, 33
    Airport, ix
    Archives, xi, xvi, 14, 27
    Bank and Trust Company, 83, 100
    Bicentennial, 100
    Board of Education, 9, 74, 78, 82, 89, 107, 115
    Board of Health, 62
    Colored Agricultural Fair Association, 40, 59, 61, 65, 93
    Colored Agricultural Fair, 49
    Commission, 91, 101
    Commissioners, 28
    Cooperative Creamery, 62, 67, 69, 74
    Court, 53, 63, 74
    Courthouse, 13, 49, **12, 74, 77–78**
    Fair, 47, **81**
    Fair Association, 67
    General Sessions Court Building, **94**
    Guidance Center, 83
    Health, Education, and Housing Facilities Board, 97

GALLATIN 200

Health Department, 54, 58, 62, 68, 112
Historical Society, xvi, 85
Hospital, 82
Industrial Board, 89
Jail, 114
Memorial Home, 67
Memorial Hospital, 73, 91–92, 97
Museum, x–xi, 91, 110, **108**
Resource Authority, ix, 5, 11, 91–92, 104, **99**
Sesquicentennial of 1937, 62, 67
Sherriff's Department, 101
Temperance Society, 30
United Way, 85
Sumner County News, 54, 57, 61, 78, 89
Sumner Farmers, 74
Sumner Female Academy, 3, 33, 38
Sumner Foundation, 111
Sumner Hall Drive, 112
Sumner Land Company, 59
Sumner Medical Society, 53
Sumner Phosphate Company, 47
Sumner Regional Medical Center, ix, xvi, 27, 109, **7, 105–6**
Sumner Regional Medical Systems, 109–10
Sumner *Times*, 89
Sumner Training School, 47
Sunbelt Container, Inc., 97
Sunset Boulevard, 72
Svoboda, Jim, v

T

Tanyard, Fry, 54
Teamsters Union, 83
Templeton, J. O., 22–23
Temporary Residence for Adolescents in Crisis, Inc., 85
Tennessean, 29
Tennessee
   Bicentennial Stamp, 111
   General Assembly, ix, 4, 28, 31, 43
   Historical Society, 36
   Power Company, 52
   State Library, xvi
   State Department of Transportation (DOT), 94, 101, 111, 113
   State Health Facilities Commission, 92
   State Highway Department, 65
Tennessee Valley Authority (TVA), 5, 10, 62–64, 71–73, 83–85, 91–92, 96, 110–11, 113
Tennessee Vocational Training Center, 82
Territory of the United States South of the River Ohio, 4
The Bud of Thought, 38
The Cumberland Farmer, 33
"The Holy City," 47
The Last Plantation, 114
The Southron, 35
Thomas, James W., v, xvi
Thomas, W. W., 16
Thompson, E. W., 20–21
Thompson, Joe H., xvi
Thomson, Kenneth, v, xvi
Three Star Certification, 108, 111–12
Three Star Community Economic Preparedness Program, 108
Tibbett, H., 17
Tomkins, Charles R., 53
Tomkins, Charles R., Jr., 68
Tomkins, Grace A.
Tomkins, J. R. A., 15
Tomkins, James S., 17
Tomkins, W. R., 17–18
Town Creek, 54, 62–63, 67, 72, 74
Trainer Metal Forming, Inc., 101
Transmontania Academy, 3, 28–29, 40
Treaty of Ghent, 5
Treaty of Versailles, 51
Trigg, John H., 16
Triple Creek Park, 111–12, **109**
Trojan Homes, 74
Trousdale, James, 4
Trousdale, Louisa, 36
Trousdale, William, 15, 36, 40, **37**
Trousdale Place, 29, 91, 111, **32, 60**

Truman, Harry, 65–66
TRW, Inc., 96
Tucson, Az., 67
Turner, E. E., 20
Turner, E. P., 62
Turner, Erskine, 61
Turner, John G., 16
Turner, Nelson, 17
Twitty, Conway, 92
Twitty City, 92

U

Union, 4, 31, 38, 40, **44**
Union Army, 13, 38–39, 110
Union Elementary School, 112
Union High School, 53, 62, 68–70, **69, 82**
Union Thanksgiving service, xv
United Auto Workers Union, 110
United Chambers of Sumner County, 108
United States
   Congress, 4, 28–29, 31, 35–36, 41, 45, 50
   Congressman, 82
   Highway 70, 6, 79
   Highway 31-E (Scottsville Pike), 104
   House, 36, 40, 106
   Pacific Fleet, 64
   Postal Service, 42, 78
   Senate, 40, 43, 45, 59, 78, 106
   Senators and Representatives, 26
   Supreme Court, 112
   Treasury Building, **ii**
United Way's Gold Achievement Award, 85
Unity Day, xv, **80**
University of Tennessee (UT) Extension Service, 71
Upper Sumner Press, 74

V

Vanderbilt University, 4
Vaughan, H. B., 15
Vena Stuart Elementary School, 112
Veterans Administration, 61–62
Veterans Memorial, 71, **110**
Veterans of Foreign Wars, 67
Veterans Wall of Honor, **111**
Victory in Europe (VE) Day, 66
Vietnam Veterans Boulevard, 110, 113
Vietnam War, 5, 80
Village Green, 96, 100
Vine Street, 72
Vinson, T. S., 19
Virginia, 54
Volunteer Box, **72**
Volunteer State Community College, ix, xvi, 3, 6, 9, 27, 82, 91, 109–10, 112, 115, **6, 105**

W

W. L. Baker's Carriage Shop, 47
W. N. Robertson & Company, 48
W. W. Fidler's Mastodon Fusee Minstrels, 45
Wade Motor Company, 67
Wallace, Angela, 23
Wallace, Bert, 12, 56, **12**
Wallace, Elizabeth, 56
Wal-Mart, 109–10
Walnut Grove, **28**
Walton, J. T., 18
Walton, John W., 17
WAMG, 74, 109
Warner, Jacob L., 15
War of 1812, 5
Warren, W. P., 20
Washington, D.C., 46, 114, **ii**
Washington, George, 54
Washington, John, 54
Watercraft, 83, 85
Water Street, 35, 43
Watkins, B., 15

Watkins, T. L., 20
WDAD, 55
Webster, Ralph, v
Welk, Lawrence, 82
Wemyss, Ellen, 114
Wemyss, William H., 71
West, Perry A., 20
West Bledsoe Street, 114
West Eastland, 6, 112
Western Europe, 65
Western Reserve Plastics, 92, 96, 111
West Franklin Street, 84
Westinghouse Corporation, 97
West Main Street, 6, 28, 41–42, 47, 50, 54, 57–58, 63, 67–69, 84
Westmoreland, Tenn., 7
West Smith Street, 101, 114
WFMG, 72
Wheatley, Ralph, 65
Whig Party, 31
WHIN, 68–69
White, James Hubert, 69
White, John J., 15
White House Utility District, 111
Whitesides, James M., 17
Wildcat, 80
Willett, Major, 110
Williams, B. A., 19
Williams, Hank, Jr., 94
Williams, Laura, 38
Williams, S. W., 20
Williams, Sam, 51
Williamson, R., 16
Williams School, 3, 51
Williams Training School, 51–52
Will-Ro Corporation, 89
Wilson, James "Curly," 13
Wilson, S. F., 19
Wilson, Sumner A., 14
Wilson County, 6, 50
Winchester, James, 28–29
Winchester, Marcus, 29
Winchester, Tenn., 6
Winchester Street, 40, 66, 74, **47**
WLAC, 68
WMRO, 109
Womack, Jim, 23
Womack, Joe, 22–23
Wood, Randy, 72, 82
Woodmen of the World, 55
Woods Ferry, 5, 55–56, 58–59, 68–69, **73**
Woods Ferry Bridge, 59
Woodson, L. M., 6, 19
Woodson, T. M., 17–18
Woodson Terrace Historic District, 110
Woodward, F. A., 20
World Trade Center, 114
World War I, 5, 27, 51, 66
World War II, 5, 64–68, **78**
Worth, T. C., 64
Wright, Don, v, xv, xvi, 23, 113, **ix**
Wright, G. B., 17
Wright, William, 16–17
WSM, 50, 55
WVCP, 91
Wynette, Tammy, 94
Wynnewood, **xi**

Y

Yale and Towne Manufacturing Company, 7, 70, 77, 79, 86, **84**
Young Men's Business Club, 62
Young Men's Christian Association (YMCA), 101
Youree, Francis, 15–16